HOW THE
MIGHTY FALL

And Why Some Companies Never Give In

JIM COLLINS

Distributed in the United States and Canada exclusively by HarperCollins Publishers Inc., 10 East 53rd Street, New York, NY 10022.

ISBN 978-0-9773264-1-9

09   10   11   12   13   DIX/RRD   5   4   3   2   1

To the late Bill Lazier,
who lives inside the thousands he touched
during his all-too-brief visit to our world

CONTENTS

ACKNOWLEDGMENTS

I owe a debt of gratitude to many people for their hand in helping this work come to life.

I thank my ChimpWorks home team for their role in this project and for their ongoing effort to keep the system running: Susan Barlow Toll for her extensive fact checking and citations, Michael Lane for his superb editing and conceptual contributions, Taffee Hightower for her happy binders and management of the critical-reader process, Judi Dunckley for her making sure everything balances (and keeping us all very afraid), Vicki Mosur Osgood for her years of service turning the ChimpWorks flywheel, and Kathy Worland-Turner for her cheerful effectiveness serving as my right arm so that I can focus on creative work and teaching.

I thank members of my research team for their contributions to this project: Robyn Bitner for her analyses and fact checking, Kyle Blackmer for his work on Merck, Brad Caldwell for his work on HP and IBM, Lauren Cujé for her work on Nordstrom, Terrence Cummings for his many projects and his contribution to the study-set selection, Todd Driver for his work on financial analyses and IBM and his fact checking, Ryan Hall for his study-set selection analyses and collection of key data, Lorilee Linfield for her work on Best Buy and Circuit City and her fact checking, Catherine Patterson for her analyses, Matthew Unangst for his study-set selection analyses and work on Xerox, and Nathaniel (Natty) Zola for ongoing analysis and criticism.

I thank my editor, Deborah Knox, for her hundreds of hours of dedicated work to challenge, edit, fact check, polish, and improve the manuscript through dozens of iterations, and for her extensive examination into Merck and Fannie Mae.

I thank my critical readers, whose intelligent critiques helped sharpen the concepts and writing immeasurably. Thank you to Bill Achtmeyer, Jerry Belle, Ed Betof, Ann S. Bowers, William P. Buchanan, Scott Cederberg, Dr. Alan G. Chute, Ken Coleman, Alan J. Dabbiere, Brian Deevy, Jeff Donnelly, Salvatore D. Fazzolari, Andrew Feiler, Claudio Fernández-Aráoz, Christopher Forman, Dick Frost, Denis Godcharles, Wayne H. Gross, Eric Hagen, Pamela Hemann, Liz Heron, John B. Hess, Frank Hightower, Phil Hodgkinson, Kimberley Hollingsworth Taylor, John A. Johnson, Alan Khazei, Betina Koski, Kevin McGarvey, Thomas W. Morris, Tom Nelson, Michael Prouting, Bobby Rao, Gloria A. Regalbuto Bentley, PhD, Jim Reid, Neville Richardson, Kevin Rumon, Kim Sanchez Rael, Dirk Schlimm, Roy Spence, Frank Sullivan, Kevin Taweel, Jean Taylor, Tom Tierney, Alan Webber, Jim Weddle, and Walter Wong. I thank Frank Sullivan also for suggesting the title *How the Mighty Fall*.

I thank Betty Grebe and Carol Krismann at the University of Colorado William M. White Business Library for their able and enthusiastic assistance, helping all my research assistants with their death marches. I thank the Center for Research in Securities Pricing (CRSP) at the University of Chicago for its quality data and excellent service. I thank Dennis Bale and Lori Drawbaugh for their professionalism and for the roving office that allows me to keep doing creative work while in transit.

I thank Frances Hesselbein and Dick Cavanagh for the invitation to speak at West Point that inspired me to dive deeply into this topic. I thank Breck England for coming up with the term "well-founded hope" as a way to describe our research findings. I thank Bob Buford for his continued insistence that I pursue questions that ignite my curiosity and for his belief that less is more. I thank Alan Wurtzel and David Maxwell for their helpful perspectives on the stages framework, and for their continued friendship and belief in our work.

I thank Peter Ginsberg for his years of support, challenge, and professionalism, and for his extraordinary ability to come up with publishing ideas that have never been tried before—and to make them work. I thank Hollis Heimbouch for her editorial instincts, her advocacy, and her willingness to join me in an adventure.

I thank Janet Brockett for her design genius and friendship.

I thank Caryn Marooney for her extraordinary wisdom and creative perspective.

I thank my friend and research colleague Morten T. Hansen, who continues to inspire and challenge me by providing critical feedback and helpful guidance.

I thank my Personal Band of Brothers for their ongoing support and inspiration, and my #1 brother, Michael Collins.

Finally, and always, I thank Joanne Ernst, my life partner and best friend, for inspiring me, for being my most severe critic, and for her unyielding belief in me. After twenty-nine years, which I consider to be a nice start to an enduring marriage, I still feel lucky every single day.

PREFACE

I feel a bit like a snake that swallowed two watermelons at the same time. I'd started this project to write only an article, a diversion to engage my pen while completing the research for my next full-sized book on what it takes to endure and prevail when the world around you spins out of control (based on a six-year research project with my colleague Morten Hansen). But the question of how the mighty fall defied the constrictions of an article and evolved into this small book. I'd considered setting this piece aside until we'd finished the turbulence book, but then the mighty began to fall, like giant dominoes crashing around us.

As I write this preface, on September 25, 2008, I'm looking out at the Manhattan skyline from a United Airlines Airbus, marveling at the cataclysmic events. Bear Stearns fell from #156 on the Fortune 500 to gone, bought out by JPMorgan Chase in a desperation deal engineered over a weekend. Lehman Brothers collapsed into bankruptcy after 158 years of growth and success.

Fannie Mae and Freddie Mac, crippled, succumbed to government conservatorship. Merrill Lynch, the symbol of bullish America, capitulated to a takeover bid. Washington Mutual tottered on the edge of becoming the largest commercial bank failure in history. The U.S. government embarked on the most extensive takeover of private assets in more than seven decades in a frenetic effort to stave off another Great Depression.

To be clear, this piece is not about the 2008 financial panic on Wall Street, nor does it have anything to say about how to fix the broken mechanisms of the capital markets. The origins of this work date back to more than three years earlier, when I became curious about why some of the greatest companies in history, including some once-great enterprises we'd researched for *Built to Last* and *Good to Great,* had fallen. The aim of this piece is to offer a research-grounded perspective of how decline can happen, even to those that appear invincible, so that leaders might have a better chance of avoiding their tragic fate.

This work is also not about gloating over the demise of once-mighty enterprises that fell, but about seeing what we can learn and apply to our own situation. By understanding the five stages of decline discussed in these pages, leaders can substantially reduce the chances of falling all the way to the bottom, tumbling from iconic to irrelevant. Decline can be avoided. The seeds of decline can be detected early. And as long as you don't fall all the way to the fifth stage, decline can be reversed. The mighty can fall, but they can often rise again.

Jim Collins
Boulder, Colorado

THE SILENT CREEP
OF IMPENDING DOOM

In the autumn of 2004, I received a phone call from Frances Hesselbein, founding president of the Leader to Leader Institute. "The Conference Board and the Leader to Leader Institute would like you to come to West Point to lead a discussion with some great students," she said.

"And who will be the students?" I asked, envisioning perhaps a group of cadets.

"Twelve U.S. Army generals, twelve CEOs, and twelve social sector leaders," explained Frances. "They'll be sitting in groups of six, two from each sector—military, business, social—and they'll really want to dialogue about the topic."

"And what's the topic?"

"Oh, it's a good one. I think you'll really like it." She paused. "America."

America? I wondered, What could I possibly teach this esteemed group about America? Then I remembered what one of my mentors, Bill Lazier, told me about effective teaching: don't try to come up with the right answers; focus on coming up with good questions.

I pondered and puzzled and finally settled upon, Is America renewing its greatness, or is America dangerously on the cusp of falling from great to good?

While I intended the question to be simply rhetorical (I believe that America carries a responsibility to continuously renew itself, and it has met that responsibility throughout its history), the West Point gathering nonetheless erupted into an intense debate. Half argued that America stood as strong as ever, while the other half contended that America teetered on the edge of decline. History shows, repeatedly, that the mighty can fall. The Egyptian Old Kingdom, the Minoans of Crete, the Chou Dynasty, the Hittite Empire, the Mayan Civilization—all fell.[1] Athens fell. Rome fell. Even Britain, which stood a century before as a global superpower, saw its position erode. Is that America's fate? Or will America always find a way to meet Lincoln's challenge to be the last best hope of Earth?

At a break, the chief executive of one of America's most successful companies pulled me aside. "I find our discussion fascinating, but I've been thinking about your question in the context of my company all morning," he mused. "We've had tremendous success in recent years, and I worry about that. And so, what I want to know is, *How would you know?*"

"What do you mean?" I asked.

"When you are at the top of the world, the most powerful nation on Earth, the most successful company in your industry, the best player in your game, your very power and success might cover up the fact that you're already on the path to decline. So, how would you know?"

The question—*How would you know?*—captured my imagination and became part of the inspiration for this piece. At our research laboratory in Boulder, Colorado, we'd already been discussing the possibility of a project on corporate decline, spurred in part by the fact that some of the great companies we'd profiled in the books *Good to Great* and *Built to Last* had subsequently lost their positions of excellence. On one level, this fact didn't cause much angst; just because a company falls doesn't invalidate what we can learn by studying that company when it was at its historical best. (See the sidebar for an explanation.) But on another level, I found myself becoming increasingly curious: How *do* the mighty fall? If some of the greatest companies in history can collapse from iconic to irrelevant, what might we learn by studying their demise, and how can others avoid their fate?

I returned from West Point inspired to turn idle curiosity into an active quest. Might it be possible to detect decline early and reverse course, or even better, might we be able to practice preventive medicine? I began to think of decline as analogous to a disease, perhaps like cancer, that can grow on the inside while you still look strong and healthy on the outside. It's not a perfect analogy; as we'll see later, organizational decline, unlike cancer, is largely self-inflicted. Still, the disease analogy might be helpful. Allow me to share a personal story to illustrate.

On a cloudless August day in 2002, my wife, Joanne, and I set out to run the long uphill haul to Electric Pass, outside Aspen, Colorado, which starts at an altitude of about 9,800 feet and ends above 13,000 feet. At about 11,000 feet, I capitulated to the thin air and slowed to a walk, while Joanne continued her uphill assault. As I emerged from tree line, where thin air limits vegetation to scruffy shrubs and hardy mountain flowers, I spotted

WHY THE FALL OF PREVIOUSLY GREAT COMPANIES DOES NOT NEGATE PRIOR RESEARCH

The principles we uncovered in prior research do not depend upon the current strength or struggles of the specific companies we studied. Think of it this way: if we studied healthy people in contrast to unhealthy people, and we derived health-enhancing principles such as sound sleep, balanced diet, and moderate exercise, would it undermine these principles if some of our previously healthy subjects started sleeping badly, eating poorly, and not exercising? Clearly, sleep, diet, and exercise would still hold up as principles of health.

Or consider this second analogy: suppose we studied the UCLA basketball dynasty of the 1960s and 1970s, which won ten NCAA championships in twelve years under coach John Wooden.[2] Also suppose that we compared Wooden's UCLA Bruins to a team at a similar school that failed to become a great dynasty during the exact same era, and that we repeated this matched-pair analysis across a range of sports teams to develop a framework of principles correlated with building a dynasty. If the UCLA basketball team were to later veer from the principles exemplified by Wooden and fail to deliver championship results on par with those achieved during the Wooden dynasty, would this fact negate the distinguishing principles of performance exemplified by the Bruins under Wooden?

Similarly, the principles in *Good to Great* were derived primarily from studying specific periods in history when the good-to-great companies showed a substantial transformation into an era of superior performance that lasted fifteen years. The research did not attempt to predict which companies would remain great after their fifteen-year run. Indeed, as this work shows, even the mightiest of companies can self-destruct.

her far ahead in a bright-red sweatshirt, running from switch-back to switchback toward the summit ridge. Two months later, she received a diagnosis that would lead to two mastectomies. I realized, in retrospect, that at the very moment she looked like the picture of health pounding her way up Electric Pass, she must have already been carrying the carcinoma. That image of Joanne, looking healthy yet already sick, stuck in my mind and gave me a metaphor.

> I've come to see institutional decline like a staged disease: harder to detect but easier to cure in the early stages, easier to detect but harder to cure in the later stages. An institution can look strong on the outside but already be sick on the inside, dangerously on the cusp of a precipitous fall.

We'll turn shortly to the research that bore this idea out, but first let's delve into a terrifying case, the rise and fall of one of the most storied companies in American business history.

ON THE CUSP, AND UNAWARE

At 5:12 a.m. on April 18, 1906, Amadeo Peter Giannini felt an odd sensation, then a violent one, a slight, almost imperceptible shift in his surroundings coupled with a distant rumble like far-away thunder or a train.[3] Pause. One second. Two seconds. Then—bang!—his house in San Mateo, California, began to pitch and shake, to, fro, up, and down. Seventeen miles north in

San Francisco, the ground liquefied underneath hundreds of buildings, while heaving spasms under more solid ground catapulted stones and facades into the streets. Walls collapsed. Gas mains exploded. Fires erupted.

Determined to find out what had happened to his fledgling company, the Bank of Italy, Giannini endured a six-hour odyssey, navigating his way into the city by train and then by foot while people streamed in the opposite direction, fleeing the conflagration. Fires swept toward his offices, and Giannini had to rescue all the imperiled cash sitting in the bank. But criminals roamed through the rubble, prompting the mayor to issue a terse proclamation: "Officers have been authorized by me to KILL any and all persons found engaged in Looting or in the Commission of Any Other Crime." With the help of two employees, Giannini hid the cash under crates of oranges on two commandeered produce wagons and made a nighttime journey back to San Mateo, where he hid the money in his fireplace. Giannini returned to San Francisco the next morning and found himself at odds with other bankers who wanted to impose up to a six-month moratorium on lending. His response: putting a plank across two barrels right in the middle of a busy pier and opening for business the very next day. "We are going to rebuild San Francisco," he proclaimed.[4]

Giannini lent to the little guy when the little guy needed it most. In return, the little guy made deposits at Giannini's bank. As San Francisco moved from chaos to order, from order to growth, from growth to prosperity, Giannini lent more to the little guy, and the little guy banked even more with Giannini. The bank gained momentum, little guy by little guy, loan by loan, deposit by deposit, branch by branch, across California, renaming itself Bank of America along the way. In October 1945, it became the largest commercial bank in the world, overtaking the venerable Chase National Bank.[5] (Note of clarification: in 1998, NationsBank acquired Bank of America and took the name; the Bank of America described here is a different company than NationsBank.)

Over the next three decades, Bank of America gained a reputation as one of the best managed corporations in America.[6] An article in the January 1980 issue of *Harvard Business Review* opened with a simple summary: "The Bank of America is perhaps best known for its size—it is the world's largest bank, with nearly 1,100 branches, operations in more than 100 countries, and total assets of about $100 billion. In the opinion of many close observers, an equally notable achievement is its quality of management . . ."[7]

Were anyone to have predicted in 1980 that in just eight years Bank of America would not only fall from its acclaimed position as one of the most successful companies in the world, but would also post some of the biggest losses in U.S. banking history, rattle the financial markets to the point of briefly depressing the U.S. dollar, watch its cumulative stock performance fall more than 80 percent behind the general stock market, face a serious takeover threat from a rival California bank, cut its dividend for the first time in fifty-three years, sell off its corporate headquarters to help meet capital requirements, see the last Giannini family board member resign in outrage, oust its CEO, bring a former CEO out of retirement to save the company, and endure a barrage of critical articles in the business press with titles like "The Incredible Shrinking Bank" and "Better Stewards (Corporate and Otherwise) Went Down on the Titanic"—were anyone to have even suggested this outcome—he or she would have been viewed as a pessimistic outlier. Yet that's exactly what happened to Bank of America.[8]

If a company as powerful and well positioned as Bank of America in the late 1970s can fall so far, so hard, so quickly, then *any* company can fall. If companies like Motorola and Circuit City—icons that had once served as paragons of excellence—can succumb to the downward forces of gravity, then no one is immune. If companies like Zenith and A&P, once the unquestioned champions in their fields, can plummet from great to irrelevant, then we should be wary about our own success.

> *Every* institution is vulnerable, no matter how great. No matter how much you've achieved, no matter how far you've gone, no matter how much power you've garnered, you are vulnerable to decline. There is no law of nature that the most powerful will inevitably remain at the top. Anyone can fall and most eventually do.

I can imagine people reading this and thinking, "Oh my goodness—we've got to change! We've got to do something bold, innovative, and visionary! We've got to get going and not let this happen to us!"

Not so fast!

In December 1980, Bank of America surprised the world with its new CEO pick. *Forbes* magazine described the process as "rather like choosing a new pope," the twenty-six directors huddled behind closed doors like cardinals in conclave.[9] You might

Bank of America
Net Income 1972–1987 (in $ Millions)

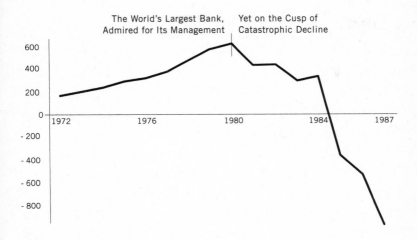

The World's Largest Bank, Admired for Its Management   Yet on the Cusp of Catastrophic Decline

think that Bank of America ultimately fell because they ended up crowning a fifty-something gentleman, a faceless bureaucrat and banker's banker who couldn't change with the times, couldn't lead with vision, couldn't make bold moves, couldn't seek new businesses and new markets.

But in fact, the board picked a vigorous, forty-one-year-old, tall, articulate, and handsome leader who told the *Wall Street Journal* that he believed the bank needed a "good kick in the fanny." Seven months after taking office, Samuel Armacost bought discount brokerage Charles Schwab, an aggressive move that pushed the edges of the Glass-Steagall Act and energized Bank of America with not only a new business, but also a cadre of irreverent entrepreneurs. Then he engineered the largest interstate banking acquisition to date in the nation's history, buying Seattle-based Seafirst Corp. He launched a $100 million crash program to blast past competitors in ATMs, allowing the bank to leap from being a laggard to boasting the largest network of ATMs in California. "We no longer have the luxury of sitting back to learn from others' mistakes before we decide on what we will do," he admonished his managers. "Let others learn from us." Here, finally, Bank of America had a *leader.*[10]

Armacost ripped apart outmoded traditions, closed branches, and ended lifetime employment. He instituted more incentive compensation. "We're trying to drive a wedge between our top performers and our nonperformers," noted one executive about the new culture.[11] He allowed Schwab's leaders to continue their practice of leasing BMWs, Porsches, and even a Jaguar, irritating traditional bankers limited to more traditional Fords, Buicks, and Chevrolets.[12] He hired a high-profile change consultant and shepherded people through a transformation process that *Business Week* likened to a religious conversion (describing the bank as "born again") and that the *Wall Street Journal* depicted as "its own version of Mao's Cultural Revolution."[13] Proclaimed Armacost, "No other financial institution has had this much change."[14] And yet, despite all this leadership, all this change, all this bold action, Bank of America fell from its net income peak of more than $600 million into a decline that culminated from 1985 to 1987 with some of the largest losses up to that point in banking history.

To be fair to Mr. Armacost, Bank of America was already poised for a downward turn before he became CEO.* My point

---

*   For an excellent account, see Gary Hector's well-written and authoritative book, *Breaking the Bank: The Decline of BankAmerica.*

is not to malign Armacost, but to show how Bank of America took a spectacular fall *despite* his revolutionary fervor. Clearly, the solution to decline lies not in the simple bromide "Change or Die"; Bank of America changed a *lot,* and nearly killed itself in the process. We need a more nuanced understanding of how decline happens, which brings us to the five stages of decline that we uncovered in our research project.

FIVE STAGES OF DECLINE

In one sense, my research colleagues and I have been studying failure and mediocrity for years, as our research methodology relies upon contrast, studying those that became great in contrast to those that did not and asking, "What's different?" But the primary focus of our quest had been on building greatness, an inherently bright and cheery topic. After my West Point experience, I wanted to turn the question around, curious to understand the decline and fall of once-great companies. I joked with my colleagues, "We're turning to the dark side."

THE RESEARCH PROCESS

We had a substantial amount of data collected from prior research studies, consisting of more than six thousand years of combined corporate history—boxes and binders of historical documents, and spreadsheets of financial information going back more than seventy years, along with substantial research chronologies and financial analyses. We expected that a rigorous screening of this data would yield a set of robust cases of companies that rose to greatness and then subsequently fell. We began with sixty major corporations from the good-to-great and built-to-last research archives, and systematically identified eleven cases that met rigorous rise-and-fall criteria at some point in their history: A&P, Addressograph, Ames Department Stores, Bank of America (before it was acquired by NationsBank), Circuit City, Hewlett-Packard (HP), Merck, Motorola, Rubbermaid, Scott Paper, and Zenith. (In Appendix 1, I've outlined the selection process.) We updated our research data archives and then examined the history of each fallen company across a range of dimensions, such as financial ratios and patterns, vision and strategy, organization, culture, leadership, technology, markets, environment, and competitive landscape. Our principal effort focused on the two-part question, What happened leading up to the point at which decline became visible and what did the company do once it began to fall?

Before we delve into the five-stage framework we derived from this analysis, allow me to make a few important research notes.

Companies in Recovery: Some of the companies in our analysis may have regained their footing by the time you read this. Merck and HP, for instance, appeared to have reversed their steep declines as we were working on this piece; whether they sustain their recovery remains to be seen, but both show improved results at the time of this writing. This brings me to an important sub-theme of this work to which we will return: just as great companies can topple, some rise again. It's important to understand that the point of our research is not to proclaim which companies are great today, or which companies will become great, remain great, or fall from greatness in the future. We study *historical* eras of performance to understand the underlying dynamics that correlate with building greatness (or losing it).

Fannie Mae and Other Financial Meltdowns of 2008: When we selected the study set of fallen companies in 2005, Fannie Mae and other financial institutions in our original database had not yet fallen far enough to qualify for this analysis. It would lack rigor to tack any of these companies onto our study as an afterthought, but at the same time, it would lack common sense to ignore the fact that some well-known financial companies (and in particular, Fannie Mae, which had been a good-to-great company) have succumbed to one of the most spectacular financial meltdowns in history. Instead of throwing these companies into the research study at the last minute because they happened to be in the news, I've included a brief commentary about Fannie Mae in Appendix 3.

Success Comparison Set: All our research studies involve a control comparison set. The critical question is *not* "What do successes share in common?" or "What do failures share in common?" The critical question is "What do we learn by studying the *contrast* between success and failure?" For this analysis, we constructed a set of "success contrasts" that had *risen* in the same industries during the era when our primary study companies *declined*. (See Appendix 2 for comparison-company selection methodology.) For an illustration, consider the chart "A Study of Contrasts" below. In the early 1970s, the two companies in this chart, Ames Department Stores and Wal-Mart (a contrast we'll discuss in a few pages), stood as almost identical twins. They had the same business model. They had similar rev-

enues and profits. They both achieved tremendous growth.
Both had strong entrepreneurial leaders at the helm. And as you
can see in the chart, both achieved exceptional investor returns
far in excess of the general stock market for more than a decade,
the two curves tracking each other very closely. But then the
curves diverge completely, one company plummeting while the
other continues to rise. Why did one fall, while the other did
not? This single contrast illustrates our comparison method.

Correlations, Not Causes: The variables we identify in our research are *correlated* with the performance patterns we study,
but we cannot claim a definitive *causal* relationship. If we could

A Study of Contrasts

Why Does One Company Fall...
And the Other Does Not?

conduct double-blind, prospective, randomized, placebo-controlled trials, we would be able to create a predictive model of corporate performance. But such experiments simply do not exist in the real world of management, and therefore it's impossible to claim cause and effect with 100-percent certainty. That said, our contrast method does give us greater confidence in our findings than if we studied only success, or only failure.

Strength of Historical Analysis: We employ a historical method, studying each company from its founding up to the end point of our investigation, focusing on specific eras of performance. We gather a range of historical materials, such as financial and annual reports, major articles published on the company, books, academic case studies, analyst reports, and industry reference materials. This is important because drawing solely upon backward-looking commentary or retrospective interviews increases the chances of fallacious conclusions. Using a well-known success story to illustrate, if we relied on only retrospective commentary about Southwest Airlines *after* it had become successful, those materials would be colored by the authors' knowledge of Southwest's success and would therefore be biased by that knowledge. For example, some retrospective accounts attribute Southwest's success to pioneering a unique and innovative airline model (in part, because the authors believe the winners must be the innovators); but in fact, a careful reading of historical documents shows that Southwest largely copied its model from Pacific Southwest Airlines in the late 1960s. If we were to rely on only retrospective accounts, we would be led astray about why Southwest became a great company.

We therefore derive our frameworks primarily from evidence *from the actual time of the events, before the outcome is known,* and we read through the evidence in chronological order, moving forward through time. Documents published at each point in time are written without foreknowledge of the company's eventual success or failure, and thereby avoid the bias of knowing the outcome. So, for instance, the materials we have on Zenith that were published in the early 1960s, when Zenith sat on top of its world, give us perspective on Zenith at that time, uncolored by the fact that Zenith would eventually fall. Interviews play a minimal part in our research method, and in this study (where people might have a strong need for self-justification), we conducted no interviews with current or recent members of management. Not that historical information is perfect—corporations can selectively exclude unhappy information from their annual reports, for example, and journalists may write with a preconceived point of view. Nor am I entirely immune from having some retrospective bias of my own, as I always know the success or failure of the company I'm studying, and I cannot erase that from my brain. But even with these limitations, our comparative historical method helps us see more clearly the factors correlated with the rise and fall of great companies.

This process of looking at historical evidence created at the time, before a company falls, yields one of the most important points to come from this work: it turns out that a company can indeed look like the picture of health on the outside yet already be in decline, dangerously on the cusp of a huge fall, just like Bank of America in 1980. And that's what makes the process of decline so terrifying; it can sneak up on you, and then— seemingly all of a sudden—you're in big trouble.

This raises a fascinating set of questions: Are there clearly distinguishable stages of decline? If so, can you spot decline early? Are there telltale markers? Can you reverse decline, and if so, how? Is there a point of no return?

THE RESULTS: A FIVE-STAGE FRAMEWORK

Surrounded by research papers at our dining room table one day, clicking away on my laptop while trying to make sense of the chronologies of decline, I commented to my wife, Joanne, "I find this much harder to get my head around than studying how companies become great." No matter how I assembled and reassembled conceptual frameworks to capture the process of decline, I'd find counterexamples and different permutations of the pattern.

Joanne suggested I look at the first line of Tolstoy's novel *Anna Karenina*. It reads, "All happy families are alike; each unhappy family is unhappy in its own way." In finishing this piece, I kept coming back to the *Anna Karenina* quote. Having studied both sides of the coin, how companies become great *and* how companies fall, I've concluded that there are more ways to fall than to become great. Assembling a data-driven framework of decline proved harder than constructing a data-driven framework of ascent.

Even so, a staged framework of how the mighty fall did emerge from the data. It's not *the* definitive framework of corporate decline—companies clearly can fall without following this framework exactly (from factors like fraud, catastrophic bad luck, scandal, and so forth)—but it is an accurate description of the cases we studied for this effort, with one slight exception (A&P had a different type of Stage 2). In the spirit of statistics professor George E. P. Box, who once wrote, "All models are wrong; some models are useful," this framework is helpful for understanding, at least in part, how great companies can fall.[15] Equally important, I believe it can be useful to leaders who seek to prevent, detect, or reverse decline.

The model consists of five stages that proceed in sequence. Let me summarize the five stages here and then provide a more detailed description of each stage in the following pages.

STAGE 1: HUBRIS BORN OF SUCCESS. Great enterprises can become insulated by success; accumulated momentum can carry an enter-

Five Stages of Decline

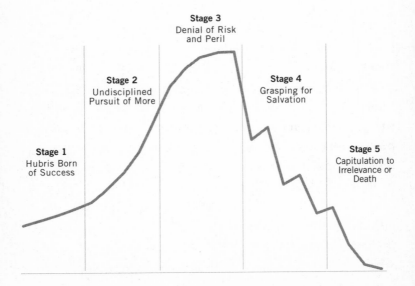

Stage 3
Denial of Risk
and Peril

Stage 2
Undisciplined
Pursuit of More

Stage 4
Grasping for
Salvation

Stage 1
Hubris Born
of Success

Stage 5
Capitulation to
Irrelevance or
Death

prise forward, for a while, even if its leaders make poor decisions or lose discipline. Stage 1 kicks in when people become arrogant, regarding success virtually as an entitlement, and they lose sight of the true underlying factors that created success in the first place. When the rhetoric of success ("We're successful because we do these specific things") replaces penetrating understanding and insight ("We're successful because we *understand why* we do these specific things and under what conditions they would no longer work"), decline will very likely follow. Luck and chance play a role in many successful outcomes, and those who fail to acknowledge the role luck may have played in their success—and thereby overestimate their own merit and capabilities—have succumbed to hubris.

STAGE 2: UNDISCIPLINED PURSUIT OF MORE. Hubris from Stage 1 ("We're so great, we can do *anything*!") leads right into Stage 2, the Undisciplined Pursuit of More—more scale, more growth, more acclaim, more of whatever those in power see as "success." Companies in Stage 2 stray from the disciplined creativity that led them to greatness in the first place, making undisciplined leaps into areas where they cannot be great or growing faster than they can achieve with excellence, or both. When an organization grows beyond its ability to fill its key seats with the right people, it has set itself up for a fall. Although complacency and resistance to change remain dangers to any successful enterprise, *overreaching* better captures how the mighty fall.

STAGE 3: DENIAL OF RISK AND PERIL. As companies move into Stage 3, internal warning signs begin to mount, yet external results remain strong enough to "explain away" disturbing data or to suggest that the difficulties are "temporary" or "cyclic" or "not that bad," and "nothing is fundamentally wrong." In Stage 3, leaders discount negative data, amplify positive data, and put a positive spin on ambiguous data. Those in power start to blame external factors for setbacks rather than accept responsibility. The vigorous, fact-based dialogue that characterizes high-performance teams dwindles or disappears altogether. When those in power begin to imperil the enterprise by taking out-sized risks and acting in a way that denies the consequences of those risks, they are headed straight for Stage 4.

STAGE 4: GRASPING FOR SALVATION. The cumulative peril and/or risks-gone-bad of Stage 3 assert themselves, throwing the enterprise into a sharp decline visible to all. The critical question is, How does its leadership respond? By lurching for a quick salvation or by getting back to the disciplines that brought about greatness in the first place? Those who grasp for salvation have fallen into Stage 4. Common "saviors" include a charismatic visionary leader, a bold but untested strategy, a radical transformation, a dramatic cultural revolution, a hoped-for blockbuster product, a "game changing" acquisition, or any number of other silver-bullet solutions. Initial results from taking dramatic action may appear positive, but they do not last.

STAGE 5: CAPITULATION TO IRRELEVANCE OR DEATH. The longer a company remains in Stage 4, repeatedly grasping for silver bullets, the more likely it will spiral downward. In Stage 5, accumulated setbacks and expensive false starts erode financial strength and individual spirit to such an extent that leaders abandon all hope of building a great future. In some cases, their leaders just sell out; in other cases, the institution atrophies into utter insignificance; and in the most extreme cases, the enterprise simply dies outright.

It is possible to skip a stage, although our research suggests that companies are likely to move through them in sequence. Some companies move quickly through the stages, while others languish for years, or even decades. Zenith, for example, took three decades to move through all five stages, whereas Rubbermaid fell from the end of Stage 2 all the way to Stage 5 in just five years. (The collapse of financial companies like Bear Stearns and Lehman Brothers that happened just as we were finishing up this work highlights the terrifying speed at which some companies fall.) An institution can stay in one stage for a long time, but then pass quickly through another stage; Ames, for instance, spent less than two years in Stage 3 but more than a decade in Stage 4 before capitulating to Stage 5. The stages can also overlap, the remnants of earlier stages playing an enabling role during later stages. Hubris, for example, can easily coincide with Undisciplined Pursuit of More, or even with Denial of Risk and Peril ("There can't be anything fundamentally wrong with *us*— we're great!"). The following diagram shows how the stages can overlap.

IS THERE A WAY OUT?

When I sent a first draft of this piece to critical readers, many commented that they found our turn to the dark side grim, even a bit depressing. And you might have the same experience as

Five Stages of Decline

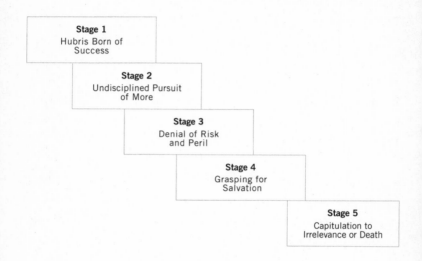

you read through the five stages of decline, absorbing story upon story of once-great companies that precipitated their own demise. It's a bit like studying train wrecks—interesting, in a morbid sort of way, but not inspiring. So, before you embark on this dark journey, allow me to provide two points of context.

First, we do ourselves a disservice by studying only success. We learn more by examining why a great company fell into mediocrity (or worse) and comparing it to a company that sustained its success than we do by merely studying a successful enterprise. Furthermore, one of the keys to sustained performance lies in understanding how greatness can be lost. Better to learn from how others fell than to repeat their mistakes out of ignorance.

Second, I ultimately see this as a work of well-founded hope. For one thing, with a roadmap of decline in hand, institutions heading downhill might be able to apply the brakes early and reverse course. For another, we've found companies that recovered—in some cases, coming back even stronger—*after having crashed down into the depths of Stage 4.* Companies like Nucor, Nordstrom, Disney, and IBM fell into the gloom at some point in their histories yet came back.

> Great companies can stumble, badly, and recover. While you can't come back from Stage 5, you can tumble into the grim depths of Stage 4 and climb out. Most companies eventually fall, and we cannot deny this fact. Yet our research indicates that organizational decline is largely self-inflicted, and recovery largely within our own control.

All companies go through ups and downs, and many show signs of Stage 1 or 2, or even Stage 3 or 4, at some point in their histories. Yet Stage 1 does not inevitably lead to Stage 5. The evidence simply does not support the notion that all companies must inevitably succumb to demise and disintegration, at least not within a 100-year time frame. Otherwise, how could you explain companies with ten to fifteen decades of achievement, companies like Procter & Gamble (P&G), 3M, and Johnson & Johnson? Just because you may have made mistakes and fallen into the stages of decline does not seal your fate. So long as you never fall all the way to Stage 5, you can rebuild a great enterprise worthy of lasting.

As you read the following pages, you might wonder, But what should we *do* if we find ourselves falling? It turns out that much of the answer lies in adhering to highly disciplined management practices, and we'll return to the question of recovery at the end of this piece. But for now, we need to descend into the darkness to better understand why the mighty fall, so that we might avoid their fate.

STAGE 1:
HUBRIS BORN OF SUCCESS

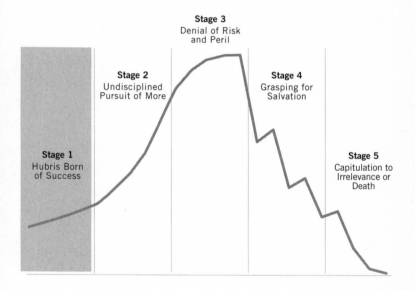

I n December 1983, the last U.S.-made Motorola car radio rolled off the manufacturing line and into Chairman Robert Galvin's hands as a reminder. Not as a sentimental memento, but as a tangible admonition to continue to develop newer technologies in an ongoing process of creative self-renewal. Motorola's history taught Galvin that it's far better to create your own future, repeatedly, than to wait for external forces to dictate your choices.[16] When the fledgling Galvin Manufacturing Corporation's first business, battery eliminators for radios, became obsolete, Paul Galvin (Robert's father) faced severe financial distress in 1929. In response, he experimented with car radios, changed the name of the company to Motorola, and started making a profit. But this near-death experience shaped Motorola's founding culture, instilling a belief that past accomplishment guarantees nothing about future success and an almost obsessive need for self-initiated progress and improvement. When Jerry Porras and I surveyed a representative sample of 165 CEOs in 1989, they selected Motorola as one of the most visionary companies in the world, and we included Motorola in our *Built to Last* research study. Amongst the eighteen visionary companies we studied at that time, Motorola received some of the highest scores on dimensions such as adherence to core values, willingness to experiment, management continuity, and mechanisms of self-improvement. We noted how Motorola pioneered Six Sigma quality programs and embraced "technology road maps" to anticipate opportunities ten years into the future.

By the mid-1990s, however, Motorola's magnificent run of success, which culminated in having grown from $5 billion to $27 billion in annual revenues in just a decade, contributed to a cultural shift from humility to arrogance. In 1995, Motorola executives felt great pride in their soon-to-be-released StarTAC cell phone; the then-smallest cell phone in the world, with its sleek clamshell design, was the first of its kind. There was just one problem: the StarTAC used analog technology just as wireless carriers began to demand digital. And how did Motorola respond? According to Roger O. Crockett, who closely covered the company for *Business Week*, one of Motorola's senior leaders dismissed the digital threat: "Forty-three million analog customers can't be wrong." [17] Then Motorola tried to strong-arm carrier companies like Bell Atlantic. If you want the hot StarTAC, explained the Motorola people, you'll need to agree to our rules: a high percentage (along the lines of 75 percent) of all your phones must be Motorola; and you must promote our phones with stand-alone displays. Bell Atlantic, irritated by this "you must" attitude, blasted back that no manufacturer would dictate how much of their product to distribute. "Do you mean to tell me that [if we don't agree to the program] you don't want to sell the StarTAC in Manhattan?" a Bell Atlantic leader reportedly challenged the Motorola executives. Motorola's arrogance gave competitors an opening, and Motorola fell from being the #1 cell phone maker in the world, at one point garnering nearly 50 percent market share, to having only 17 percent share by 1999.[18] Motorola's fall from greatness began with Stage 1, Hubris Born of Success.

ARROGANT NEGLECT

Dating back to ancient Greece, the concept of hubris is defined as excessive pride that brings down a hero, or alternatively (to paraphrase classics professor J. Rufus Fears), outrageous arrogance that inflicts suffering upon the innocent.[19] Motorola began 2001 with 147,000 employees; by the end of 2003, the number dropped to 88,000—nearly 60,000 jobs gone.[20] As Motorola de-

scended through the stages of decline, shareholders also suf-
fered as stock returns fell more than 50 percent behind the
market from 1995 to 2005.[21]

> We will encounter multiple forms of hubris in our journey through
> the stages of decline. We will see hubris in undisciplined leaps
> into areas where a company cannot become the best. We will
> see hubris in a company's pursuit of growth beyond what it can
> deliver with excellence. We will see hubris in bold, risky deci-
> sions that fly in the face of conflicting or negative evidence. We
> will see hubris in denying even the possibility that the enterprise
> could be at risk, imperiled by external threats or internal erosion.
> And we will encounter one of the most insidious forms of hubris:
> arrogant neglect.

In October 1995, *Forbes* magazine ran a laudatory story about
Circuit City's CEO. Under his leadership, Circuit City had grown
more than 20 percent per year, multiplying the size of the company nearly ten times in a decade. How to keep the growth
going? After all, as *Forbes* commented, in the end every market
becomes mature, and this energetic CEO had "no intention of
sitting around and waiting for his business to be overwhelmed
by the competition."[22] And so Circuit City sought The Next Big
Thing. The company had already piloted CarMax, a visionary
application of the company's superstore expertise to the used
car business. Circuit City also became enamored with an adventure called Divx. Using a special DVD player, customers would
be able to "rent" a DVD for as long as they liked before playing

it, using an encryption system to unlock the DVD for viewing. The advantage: not having to return a DVD to the video store before having had a chance to watch it.[23]

In late 1998, the *Wall Street Transcript* interviewed Circuit City's CEO. There came a telling moment when the interviewer asked what investors should worry about at Circuit City. "[Investors] can be fairly relaxed about our ability to run the business well," he replied. Then he felt compelled to add, "I think there has been some investor sentiment . . . that our CarMax endeavor and our Divx endeavor is taking attention away from our Circuit City business. I'd refer . . . [to] our 44 percent earnings growth in the Circuit City business in the first half of the year." He concluded, "This is a company that's in great shape."[24]

Yet Circuit City plummeted through all five stages of decline. Profit margins eroded and return on equity atrophied from nearly 20 percent in the mid-1990s to single digits, leading to the company's first loss in more than a quarter of a century. And on November 10, 2008, Circuit City announced that it had filed for bankruptcy.

Circuit City originally made the leap from good to great, a process that began to gain momentum in the early 1970s, under the inspired leadership of Alan Wurtzel. As with most climbs to greatness, it involved sustained, cumulative effort, like turning a giant, heavy flywheel: each push builds upon previous work, compounding the investment of effort—days, weeks, months, and years of work—generating momentum, from one turn to ten, from ten to a hundred, from a hundred to a thousand, from a thousand to a million. Once an organization gets one flywheel going, it might create a second or third flywheel. But to remain successful in any given area of activity, you have to keep pushing with as much intensity as when you first began building that flywheel, exactly what Circuit City did not do. Circuit City in decline exemplifies a cycle of arrogant neglect that goes like this:

1. You build a successful flywheel.
2. You succumb to the notion that new opportunities will sustain your success better than your primary flywheel, either because you face an impending threat or because you find other opportunities more exciting (or perhaps you're just bored).
3. You divert your creative attention to new adventures and fail to improve your primary flywheel as if your life depended on it.
4. The new ventures fail outright, siphon off your best creative energy, or take longer to succeed than expected.
5. You turn your creative attention back to your primary flywheel only to find it wobbling and losing momentum.

A core business that meets a fundamental human need—and one at which you've become best in the world—rarely becomes obsolete. In this analysis of decline, only one company, Zenith, fell largely because it stayed focused on its core business too long and failed to confront its impending demise. Furthermore, in 60 percent of our matched-pairs, the success-contrast company paid greater attention to improving and evolving its core business than the fallen company during the relevant era of comparison.

My point here is not that you should never evolve into new arenas or that Circuit City made a mistake by investing in CarMax or Divx. Creating CarMax required an impressive leap of imagination; Circuit City invented an entirely new business concept, doing for used cars what it had done for consumer electronics (bringing a professional chain-store approach to an industry that had previously been unprofessional and fragmented).[25] Indeed, Circuit City would have done well to keep CarMax rather than sell it. And with Divx, while the idea ultimately failed in the marketplace, it can be viewed as a relatively small experiment that just didn't work in the end, a positive example of the *Built to Last* principle "Try a Lot of Stuff and Keep What Works." The real lesson is that Circuit City left itself exposed by not revitalizing its electronics superstores with as much passion and intensity as when it first began building that business two decades earlier. The great irony is that one of its biggest opportunities for continued growth and success lay in its core business, and the proof rests in two words: Best Buy.

In 1981, a tornado touched down in Roseville, Minnesota, blasting to pieces the showroom of the local Sound of Music store. Customers hurled themselves away from the windows as shards of glass and splintered wood flew about in the gale. Luckily, the storeroom remained largely undamaged, leaving founder Richard Schulze with boxes of stereos and TVs, but no storefront. A resourceful entrepreneur, he decided to throw a "Tornado Sale" in the parking lot. He spent his entire marketing budget on a local ad blitz that created a two-mile traffic jam as droves of customers converged on the lot. Schulze realized that he'd stumbled upon a great concept: advertise like crazy, have lots of name-brand stuff to sell in a no-frills setting (albeit a step up from a parking lot), and offer low prices. Based on his discovery, he invested all his money into creating a consumer electronics superstore that he dubbed Best Buy.[26]

From 1982 to 1988, Best Buy opened forty superstores (what it called its Concept I stores) in the Midwest. In 1989, after systematically asking customers what would make for a better experience, Best Buy created its Concept II store model, which replaced a commission-driven sales culture with a consultative help-the-customer-find-the-best-answer culture.[27] In 1995, Best Buy created Concept III superstores chock-full of snazzy ways to learn about products—touchscreen information kiosks, simulated car interiors for checking out sound systems, CD listening posts to sample music, "fun & games" areas for testing video games—and then in 1999 moved on to Concept IV stores, designed to help customers navigate the confusing myriad of new electronics products flooding the market. Then it evolved yet again in 2002, and in 2003 added Geek Squads to help customers baffled by technology.[28]

We found little evidence that Circuit City senior leaders took seriously the threat from Best Buy until the late 1990s. Yet if Circuit City had invested as much creative energy into making its superstore business a superior alternative to Best Buy and had captured half of Best Buy's growth from 1997 (when the companies had the same revenues) to 2006, Circuit City would have grown to nearly *twice* the revenues it actually achieved during that period.[29] But instead, Best Buy eclipsed Circuit City by more than 2.5 times, in both revenues and profit per employee. Every dollar invested in Best Buy in 1995 and held to 2006 outperformed a dollar invested in Circuit City by four times.[30]

To disrespect the potential remaining in your primary flywheel—
or worse, to neglect that flywheel out of boredom while you turn
your attention to The Next Big Thing in the arrogant belief that its
success will continue almost automatically—is hubris. And even
if you face the impending demise of a core business, that's still
no excuse to let it just run on autopilot. Exit definitively or renew
obsessively, but do not ever neglect a primary flywheel.

If you're struggling with the tension between continuing
your commitment to what made you successful and living in
fear about what comes next, ask yourself two questions:

1. Does your primary flywheel face inevitable demise
   within the next five to ten years due to forces outside
   your control—will it become impossible for it to remain
   best in the world with a robust economic engine?
2. Have you lost passion for your primary flywheel?

If you answer no to both these questions, then continue to push
your primary flywheel with as much imagination and fanatical
intensity as you did when you first began. (Of course, you *also*
need to continually experiment with new ideas, both as a mechanism to stimulate progress and as a hedge against an uncertain
future.)

This does not mean static, unimaginative replication. Quite
the opposite: it means never-ending creative renewal, just as
Best Buy moved from Concept I to Concept II to Concept III and

beyond. It's like being an artist. Picasso didn't renew himself by abandoning painting and sculpture to become a novelist or a banker; he painted his entire life yet progressed through distinct creative phases—from his Blue Period to cubism to surrealism—*within* his primary activity. Beethoven didn't "reinvent" himself by abandoning music for poetry or painting; he remained first and foremost a composer. But neither did he just write the Third Symphony nine times.

CONFUSING WHAT AND WHY

Like an artist who pursues both enduring excellence *and* shocking creativity, great companies foster a productive tension between continuity *and* change. On the one hand, they adhere to the principles that produced success in the first place, yet on the other hand, they continually evolve, modifying their approach with creative improvements and intelligent adaptation. Best Buy understood this idea better than Circuit City, when it kept morphing its superstores yet did so in a manner consistent with the primary insight that produced success in the first place (customers really like having lots of name-brand stuff in an easy-to-navigate, low-price, and friendly environment). When institutions fail to distinguish between current practices and the enduring principles of their success, and mistakenly fossilize around their practices, they've set themselves up for decline.

When George Hartford lay on his deathbed in 1957, he summoned his longtime loyal aide, Ralph Burger, and pleaded as his dying wish, "Take care of the organization."[31] The Hartford brothers (Mr. John and Mr. George) dedicated their lives to building the Great Atlantic & Pacific Tea Company (A&P) after taking it over from their father. Burger, himself nearly seventy years old, spent decades as a chief confidant and pursued his solemn oath to preserve and protect the Hartford legacy with fundamentalist zeal. He clothed himself in the authority of the Hartford brothers, and not just figuratively; according to William Walsh's account *The Rise and Decline of The Great Atlantic & Pacific Tea Company*, Burger took to wearing Mr. John's actual clothes, saying, "John would not have wanted those famous grey suits to go to waste." [32] Insulated by A&P's comfortable position as the largest retailing organization in the world, Burger believed that "taking care of the organization" meant preserving its specific practices and methods; as late as 1973, Mr. John's office remained exactly as it had been two decades earlier, right down to the same coat hangers hanging in the same place in the closet. [33]

During the Burger era, A&P's arrogant stance that "we will continue to keep things just the way they are and we will continue to be successful because—well, we're A&P!" left it vulnerable to new store formats developed by companies like Kroger. Burger failed to ask the fundamental question, *Why* was A&P successful in the first place? Not the specific practices and strategies that worked in the past, but the fundamental *reasons* for success. It retained its aging Depression-generation customers but became utterly irrelevant to a new generation. As one industry observer quipped, "Like the undertaker, A&P could have said every time a hearse went by, 'There goes another customer.'" [34]

The point here is not as simple as "they failed because they didn't change." As we'll see in the later stages of decline, companies that change constantly but without any consistent rationale will collapse just as surely as those that change not at all. There's nothing inherently wrong with adhering to specific practices and strategies (indeed, we see tremendous consistency over time in great companies), but only if you comprehend the underlying *why* behind those practices, and thereby see when to keep them and when to change them.

Now you might be wondering, "How do you know if you're right about the underlying causes of your success?" The best leaders we've studied never presume that they've reached ultimate understanding of all the factors that brought them success. For one thing, they retain a somewhat irrational fear that perhaps their success stems in large part from luck or fortuitous circumstance. Compare the downside of two approaches:

APPROACH 1: Suppose you discount your own success ("We might have been just really lucky or were in the right place at the right time or have been living off momentum or have been operating without serious competition") and thereby worry incessantly about how to make yourself stronger and better positioned for the day your good luck runs out. What's the downside if you're wrong? Minimal; if you're wrong, you'll just be that much stronger by virtue of your disciplined approach.

APPROACH 2: Suppose you attribute success to your own superior qualities ("We deserve success because we're so good, so smart, so innovative, so amazing"). What's the downside if you're wrong? Significant; if you're wrong, you just might find yourself surprised and unprepared when you wake up to discover your vulnerabilities too late.

Like inquisitive scientists, the best corporate leaders we've researched remain students of their work, relentlessly asking questions—why, why, why?—and have an incurable compulsion to vacuum the brains of people they meet. To be a knowing person ("I already know everything about why this works, and let me tell you") differs fundamentally from being a *learning* person. The "knowing people" can set companies on the path to decline in two ways. First, they can become dogmatic about their specific practices ("We know we're successful because we do these specific things, and we see no reason to question them") as we saw with A&P. Second, they can overreach, moving into sectors or growing to a scale at which the original success factors no longer apply ("We've been so successful that we can really go for the big bet, the huge growth, the gigantic leap to exciting new adventures"), as we'll see in the following contrast between two companies, one that became the largest company in America and the other, its competitor, that died.

In the late 1950s, a small, unknown company had a Very Big Idea: "to bring discount retailing to rural and small town areas." [35] It became one of the first companies to bet its future on this concept, and it built a substantial early lead by adopting everyday low prices for everything, not just specific lure-the-customer items. [36] Its visionary leader created an ethos of partnership with his people, engineered sophisticated information systems, and cultivated a performance-driven culture, with

store managers reviewing weekly scorecards at 5 a.m. every
Monday morning. Not only did the company decimate Main
Street stores in small towns, but it also learned how to beat
its primary competitor, Kmart, in head-to-head competition.[37]
Every dollar invested in its stock at the start of 1970 and held
through 1985 grew more than six *thousand* percent.[38]

So, now, what is the company?

If you answered Wal-Mart, good guess. But wrong.

The answer is Ames Department Stores.

Ames began in 1958 with the same idea that eventually made
Wal-Mart famous and did so four years before Sam Walton
opened his first Wal-Mart store.[39] Over the next two decades,
both companies built seemingly unstoppable momentum, Wal-
Mart growing in the mid-South and Ames in the Northeast.
From 1973 to 1986, Ames's and Wal-Mart's stock performances
roughly tracked each other, with both companies generating
returns over nine times the market.[40]

So where is Ames at the time of this writing, in 2008?

Dead. Gone. Never to be heard from again. Wal-Mart is alive
and well, #1 on the Fortune 500 with $379 billion in annual
revenues.

What happened? What distinguished Wal-Mart from Ames?

A big part of the answer lies in Walton's deep humility and
learning orientation. In the late 1980s, a group of Brazilian investors bought a discount retail chain in South America. After
purchasing the company, they figured they'd better learn more
about discount retailing, so they sent off letters to about ten
CEOs of American retailing companies, asking for a meeting
to learn about how to run the new company better. All the

CEOs either declined or neglected to respond, except one: Sam Walton.[41]

When the Brazilians deplaned at Bentonville, Arkansas, a kindly, white-haired gentleman approached them, inquiring, "Can I help you?"

"Yes, we're looking for Sam Walton."

"That's me," said the man. He led them to his pickup truck, and the Brazilians piled in alongside Sam's dog, Ol' Roy.

Over the next few days, Walton barraged the Brazilians with question after question about their country, retailing in Latin America, and so on, often while standing at the kitchen sink washing and drying dishes after dinner. Finally, the Brazilians realized, Walton—the founder of what may well become the world's first trillion-dollar-per-year corporation—sought first and foremost to learn from them, not the other way around.

Wal-Mart's success worried Walton. He fretted over how to instill his sense of purpose and humble inquisitiveness into the company beyond his own lifetime, as Wal-Mart grew to hundreds of billions of dollars of annual revenue. Part of his answer for how to stave off hubris came in handing the company to an equally inquisitive, self-deprecating CEO, the quiet and low-profile David Glass. Most people outside retailing do not recognize the name David Glass, which is exactly how Glass would want it. He learned from Walton that Wal-Mart does not exist for the aggrandizement of its leaders; it exists for its customers. Glass fervently believed in Wal-Mart's core purpose (to enable people of average means to buy more of the same things previously available only to wealthier people) and in the need to stay true to that purpose. And like Walton, he relentlessly sought better ways for Wal-Mart to pursue its purpose. He kept hiring great people, building the culture, and expanding into new arenas (from groceries to electronics) while adhering to the principles that made Wal-Mart great in the first place.

Quite a contrast to Ames. Whereas Walton engineered a smooth transition of power to a homegrown insider who deeply understood the drivers of Wal-Mart's success and exemplified the cultural DNA right down to his tippy toes, Ames's CEO Herb Gilman brought in an outsider as his successor, a visionary leader who boldly redefined the company.[42] While Wal-Mart maintained its near-religious fanaticism about its core values, purpose, and culture, Ames did the opposite in its quest for quick growth, catapulting itself right into Stage 2, Undisciplined Pursuit of More, to which we will turn next.

MARKERS FOR STAGE 1

At the end of each of the first four stages, I'll summarize the stage with a series of markers. Not every marker shows up in every case of decline, and the presence of a marker does not necessarily mean that you have a disease, but it does indicate an increased possibility that you're in that stage of decline. You can use these markers as a self-diagnostic checklist. Some of the markers listed have little or no text dedicated to them in the preceding pages, for the simple reason that they're highly self-explanatory.

- **SUCCESS ENTITLEMENT, ARROGANCE:** Success is viewed as "deserved," rather than fortuitous, fleeting, or even hard earned in the face of daunting odds; people begin to believe that success will continue almost no matter what the organization decides to do, or not to do.

- **NEGLECT OF A PRIMARY FLYWHEEL:** Distracted by extraneous threats, adventures, and opportunities, leaders neglect a primary flywheel, failing to renew it with the same creative intensity that made it great in the first place.

- **"WHAT" REPLACES "WHY":** The rhetoric of success ("We're successful because we do these specific things") replaces understanding and insight ("We're successful because we understand *why* we do these specific things and under what conditions they would no longer work").

- **DECLINE IN LEARNING ORIENTATION:** Leaders lose the inquisitiveness and learning orientation that mark those truly great individuals who, no matter how successful they become, maintain a learning curve as steep as when they first began their careers.

- **DISCOUNTING THE ROLE OF LUCK:** Instead of acknowledging that luck and fortuitous events might have played a helpful role, people begin to presume that success is due entirely to the superior qualities of the enterprise and its leadership.

STAGE 2:
UNDISCIPLINED
PURSUIT OF MORE

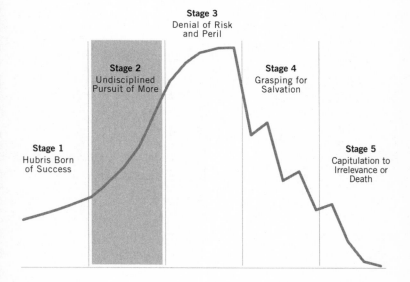

In 1988, Ames bought Zayre department stores, with self-proclaimed expectations to more than double the size of the company in a single year.[43] You cannot do a 0.2 or a 0.5 or a 0.7 acquisition. The decision is binary. You either do the acquisition or you don't, one or zero, no in between. And if that acquisition turns out to be a mistake, you cannot undo the decision. Big mergers or acquisitions that do not fit with your core values or that undermine your culture or that run counter to that at which you've proven to be best in the world or that defy economic logic—big acquisitions taken out of bravado rather than penetrating insight and understanding—can bring you down.

In Ames's case, the Zayre acquisition destroyed the momentum built over three decades. While Wal-Mart continued to focus first on rural and small town areas before making an evolutionary migration into more urban settings, the Zayre acquisition revolutionized Ames, making it a significant urban player overnight. And while Wal-Mart remained obsessed with offering everyday low prices on all brands all the time, Ames dramatically changed its strategy with Zayre, which relied on special loss-leader promotions. Ames more than doubled its revenues from 1986 to 1989, but much of its growth simply did not fit with the strategic insight that produced Ames's greatness in the first place. From 1986 through 1992, Ames's cumulative stock returns fell 98 percent as the company plunged into bankruptcy.[44] Ames emerged from bankruptcy, but never regained momentum and liquidated in 2002.[45] Meanwhile, Wal-Mart continued its relentless march across the United States—step by step, store by store, region by region—until it reached the Northeast and killed Ames with the very same business model that Ames pioneered in the first place.[46]

OVERREACHING, NOT COMPLACENCY

We anticipated that most companies fall from greatness because they become complacent—they fail to stimulate innovation, they fail to initiate bold action, they fail to ignite change, they just become lazy—and watch the world pass them by. It's a plausible theory, with a problem: it doesn't square with our data. Certainly, any enterprise that becomes complacent and refuses to change or innovate will eventually fall. But, and this is the surprising point, the companies in our analysis showed little evidence of complacency when they fell. Overreaching much better explains how the once-invincible self-destruct.

Only one case showed strong evidence of complacency: A&P. (A&P followed a pattern of Hubris → Complacency → Denial → Grasping for Salvation.) In every other case, we found tremendous energy—stimulated by ambition, creativity, aggression and/or fear—in Stage 2. (See Appendix 4.A for an evidence table.) We even found substantial innovation during this stage, which eliminated the hypothesis that the fall of a great company is necessarily preceded by a decline in innovation. In only three of eleven cases did we find significant evidence that the company failed to innovate during the early stages of decline (A&P, Scott Paper, and Zenith). Motorola increased its number of patents from 613 to 1,016 from 1991 to 1995, and stated about its patent productivity, "We rank No. 3 in the United States."[47] Merck patented 1,933 new compounds from 1996 to 2002 (the best performance in the industry, 400 ahead of second place) yet was already in the stages of decline.[48] In 1999, HP launched its "Invent" campaign and nearly doubled patent applications in two years, just as it spiraled into Stage 4 decline.[49]

And then there's the terrifying demise of Rubbermaid. In the early 1990s, two Rubbermaid executives visited the antiquities section of the British Museum. The ancient Egyptians "used a lot of kitchen utensils, some of which were very nice," said one of the executives in a *Fortune* magazine feature, designs so nice that he came away from the museum with eleven ideas for new products. "The Egyptians had some really neat ideas for food storage," echoed the other. "They had clever little levers that made it easy to take the lids off wooden vessels." [50]

Eleven ideas from one visit to the British Museum might sound like a lot, but not when you consider that Rubbermaid aimed to introduce at least one new product *per day*, seven days a week, 365 days per year, while entering a new product category every twelve to eighteen months. [51] "Our vision is to grow," proclaimed Rubbermaid's CEO in a 1994 statement that outlined goals for "leap growth." Growth would come from doing lots of new stuff, all at the same time—new markets, new acquisitions, new geographies, new technologies, new joint ventures, and above all, hundreds of new product innovations per year. "Exhibit A in the case for innovation," wrote *Fortune* about Rubbermaid's climb to become the #1 "Most Admired Company" in America, more innovative than 3M, more innovative than Apple, more innovative than Intel. [52]

Choking on nearly one thousand new products introduced in three years, hammered on one side by raw materials costs that nearly doubled in eighteen months, and pressed on the other side by its ambitious growth targets, Rubbermaid began to fray at the edges, failing at basic mechanics like controlling costs and filling orders on time. [53] From 1994 to 1998, Rubbermaid raced through the stages of decline so rapidly that it should terrify anyone who has enjoyed a burst of success. In the fourth quarter of 1995, Rubbermaid reported its first loss in decades. The company eliminated nearly six thousand product variations, closed nine plants, and wiped out 1,170 jobs. It also made one of the largest acquisitions in its history, recast incentive compensation, and initiated a radical marketing bet on the Internet as "a renaissance tool." [54] Yet Rubbermaid continued to sputter, embarked on a second major restructuring in a little over two years, and on October 21, 1998, sold out to Newell Corporation, forfeiting forever the chance to come back as a great company. [55] As Rubbermaid realized too late, innovation can fuel growth, but frenetic innovation—growth that erodes consistent tactical excellence—can just as easily send a company cascading through the stages of decline.

This provokes a question: Why do we instinctively point to complacency and lack of innovation as a dominant pattern of decline, despite evidence to the contrary? I can offer two answers. First, those who build great companies have drive and passion and intensity and an incurable itch for progress somewhere in their DNA to begin with; if we studied companies that never excelled, those that fell from so-so to bad, we might see a different pattern. Second, perhaps people want to attribute the fall of others to a character flaw they don't see in themselves rather than face the frightening possibility that they might be just as vulnerable. "They fell because they became lazy and self-satisfied, but since *I* work incredibly hard and *I'm* willing to change and innovate and lead with passion, well, then *I* don't have that character flaw. *I'm* immune. It can't happen to *me!*" But of course, catastrophic decline can be brought about by driven, intense, hard-working, and creative people. It's hard to argue that the primary cause of the Wall Street meltdowns of 2008 lay in a lack of drive or ambition; if anything, people went too far—too much risk, too much leverage, too much financial innovation, too much aggressive opportunism, too much growth.

OBSESSED WITH GROWTH

In his 1995 annual letter to shareholders, Merck's chairman and CEO Ray Gilmartin delineated the company's #1 business objective: being a top-tier growth company. Not profitability, not breakthrough drugs, not scientific excellence, not research-driven R&D, not productivity (although Gilmartin did highlight these as essential elements of Merck's strategy), but one overriding business objective: growth. Merck's drive for growth remained remarkably consistent for the next seven years. The opening line of the chairman's letter in the 2000 annual report stated simply, "As a company, Merck is totally focused on growth."

Merck's public commitments to achieve audacious growth seemed odd, given the facts. Five Merck drugs with annual revenues of nearly $5 billion would lose their U.S. patent protection in the early 2000s.[56] Generic copycat drugs, an increasing force in the pharmaceutical industry, would curtail Merck's pricing power, wiping out billions in profitable sales. Moreover, Gilmartin faced a significantly larger revenue base upon which to achieve growth than his predecessor, Roy Vagelos. It's one thing to develop enough new drugs to deliver growth on a base of approximately $5 billion, as Vagelos did in the late 1980s, but entirely another to develop enough new drugs to fuel the same or faster growth on a base of more than $25 billion, as Gilmartin faced in the late 1990s. And for a company like Merck that relied primarily upon scientific discovery, growth would be increasingly difficult to attain; according to a Harvard Business School case study, the probabilities of any new molecule creating a profitable return were about 1 in 15,000.[57]

"But if Gilmartin is worried," wrote *Business Week* in 1998, "he doesn't show it."[58] And why would Merck feel so confident about its prospects? The second paragraph of the chairman's message in the 1998 annual report reveals part of the answer: Vioxx.[59] In 1999, Merck received FDA approval and launched Vioxx, touting it as a potentially huge blockbuster, emblazoning the front cover of its annual report with "Vioxx: Our biggest, fastest and best launch ever."[60]

In March 2000, preliminary results of a study of more than eight thousand rheumatoid arthritis patients demonstrated Vioxx's powerful advantage: a painkiller with fewer gastrointestinal side effects than the painkiller naproxen. But the study also raised troubling, albeit inconclusive, questions about Vioxx's safety, indicating that those taking naproxen had lower rates of "cardiovascular thrombotic events" (in lay terms, heart attacks and strokes) than the Vioxx group.[61] Since the study was designed without a placebo-taking control group, the results could be interpreted a number of ways: naproxen lowers cardiovascular risk, Vioxx increases cardiovascular risk, or some combination of the two. Naproxen, like aspirin, has what scientists call "cardioprotective" effects, and Merck concluded that the difference in the frequency of cardiovascular events was "most likely due to the effects of naproxen."[62]

By 2002, Vioxx sales had climbed to $2.5 billion, and by 2004 it had generated more than one hundred million prescriptions in the United States, including one for Gilmartin's wife.[63] Meanwhile, outside critics continued to raise questions about Vioxx.[64] Merck countered with interim findings from studies involving twenty-eight thousand patients that did not show higher rates of cardiovascular risk for those taking Vioxx.[65]

Then in mid-September 2004, the safety monitors for the Vioxx study of colon-polyp prevention received Federal Express deliveries containing alarming data. According to Brooke Masters and Marc Kaufman, who covered the story for the *Washington Post*, the safety-monitor team pored over the data for several days and couldn't escape a frightening conclusion, later summarized in Merck's annual report: "there was an increased relative risk for confirmed cardiovascular events, such as heart attack and stroke, beginning after 18 months of treatment in the patients taking Vioxx compared to those taking placebo."[66] The study's steering committee halted the trials, sending shock waves throughout Merck.[67] "It was totally out of the blue," Gilmartin told the *Boston Globe* when he learned of the steering committee's conclusion. "I was stunned."[68] To his credit, Gilmartin made a decision, clear and unequivocal; on September 30, within a week of when he learned of the new data, Merck voluntarily removed Vioxx from the market. Merck's stock dropped from $45 to $33, chopping off more than $25 billion in market capitalization in one day, and shareholders lost another $15 billion as its stock dropped below $26 in early November—$40 billion in market valuation gone in six weeks.[69]

The final perspective on Vioxx—of the courts, of the marketplace, of investors, of the medical and scientific community, of the general public—continues to evolve as I write these words. My point here is not to argue that Merck leaders were villains seeking profits at the expense of patient lives or, conversely, that they were heroes who courageously removed a hugely profitable product without anyone requiring that they do so. Nor is my point that Merck made a mistake by pursuing a blockbuster; Merck has pursued blockbusters for decades, often with great success and benefit to patients. My point, rather, is that Merck committed itself to attaining such huge growth that Vioxx *had* to be a blockbuster, which, in turn, positioned the company for a gigantic fall if Vioxx failed to live up to its promise.

> If Merck had underpromised and overdelivered as a consistent practice, we might not be writing about Merck's spectacular tumble. But that's the problem; hubris can lead to making brash commitments for more and more and more. And then one day, just when you've elevated expectations too far, you fall. Hard.

Merck's quest for growth subtly diluted the power of Merck's purpose-driven philosophy that made the company great in the first place. In 1950, George Merck II articulated a visionary business purpose: "We try never to forget that medicine is for the people. It is not for the profits. The profits follow, and if we have remembered that, they have never failed to appear."[70] It's not that Merck abandoned this core purpose (indeed, Gilmartin drew inspiration from it when he removed Vioxx from the market), so much as it appears to have been relegated to more of a background role, a constraint on growth rather than the company's fundamental driving force.

All three companies from *Built to Last* that fell in this analysis—Merck, Motorola, and HP—pursued outsized growth to their detriment. Their founders had built their companies upon noble purposes far beyond just making money. George Merck II passionately sought to preserve and improve human life. Paul Galvin obsessed over the idea of continuous renewal through unleashing human creativity. Bill Hewlett and David Packard believed that HP existed to make technical contributions, with profit serving as only a means and measure of achieving that purpose. George Merck II, Paul Galvin, Bill Hewlett, and David Packard—they viewed expanding and increasing scale not as the end goal, but as a residual *result*, an inevitable outcome, of pursuing their core purpose. Later generations forgot this lesson. Indeed, they inverted it.

Public corporations face incessant pressure from the capital markets to grow as fast as possible, and we cannot deny this fact. But even so, we've found in all our research that those who resisted the pressures to succumb to unsustainable short-term growth delivered better long-term results by Wall Street's *own* definition of success, namely cumulative returns to investors. Those who built the great companies in our research distinguished between share *value* and share *price*, between share*holders* and share*flippers*, and recognized that their responsibility lay in building shareholder value, not in maximizing shareflipper price. The greatest leaders do seek growth—growth in performance, growth in distinctive impact, growth in creativity, growth in people—but they do not succumb to growth that undermines long-term value. And they certainly do not confuse growth with excellence. Big does not equal great, and great does not equal big.

BREAKING PACKARD'S LAW

To be clear, the problems of Stage 2 stem not from growth per se, but from the *undisciplined* pursuit of more. While the Merck story highlights the perils of growth obsession, we can see Stage 2 behavior in any number of other forms. Discontinuous leaps into arenas for which you have no burning passion is undisciplined. Taking action inconsistent with your core values is undisciplined. Investing heavily in new arenas where you cannot attain distinctive capability, better than your competitors, is undisciplined. Launching headlong into activities that do not fit with your economic or resource engine is undisciplined. Addiction to scale is undisciplined. To neglect your core business while you leap after exciting new adventures is undisciplined. To use the organization primarily as a vehicle to increase your own personal success—more wealth, more fame, more power— at the expense of its long-term success is undisciplined. To compromise your values or lose sight of your core purpose in pursuit of growth and expansion is undisciplined.

One of the most damaging manifestations of Stage 2 comes in breaking "Packard's Law." (We named this law after David Packard, cofounder of HP, inspired by his insight that a great company is more likely to die of indigestion from too much opportunity than starvation from too little.[71] Ironically, as we'll see when we get to Stage 4, HP itself later broke Packard's Law.) Packard's Law states that no company can consistently grow revenues faster than its ability to get enough of the right people to implement that growth and still become a great company. Though we have discussed Packard's Law in our previous work, as we looked through the lens of decline we gained a more profound understanding: if a great company consistently grows revenues faster than its ability to get enough of the right people to implement that growth, it will not simply stagnate; it will fall.

Any exceptional enterprise depends first and foremost upon having self-managed and self-motivated people—the #1 ingredient for a culture of discipline. While you might think that such a culture would be characterized by rules, rigidity, and bureaucracy, I'm suggesting quite the opposite. If you have the right people, who accept responsibility, you don't need to have a lot of senseless rules and mindless bureaucracy in the first place! (For a brief discussion of the right people for key seats, see Appendix 5.)

But a Stage 2 company can fall into a vicious spiral. You break Packard's Law and begin to fill key seats with the wrong people; to compensate for the wrong people's inadequacies, you institute bureaucratic procedures; this, in turn, drives away the right people (because they chafe under the bureaucracy or cannot tolerate working with less competent people or both); this then invites more bureaucracy to compensate for having more of the wrong people, which then drives away more of the right people; and a culture of bureaucratic mediocrity gradually replaces a culture of disciplined excellence. When bureaucratic rules erode an ethic of freedom and responsibility within a framework of core values and demanding standards, you've become infected with the disease of mediocrity.

If I were to pick one marker above all others to use as a warning sign, it would be a declining proportion of key seats filled with the right people. Twenty-four hours a day, 365 days a year, you should be able to answer the following questions: What are the key seats in your organization? What percentage of those seats can you say with confidence are filled with the right people? What are your plans for increasing that percentage? What are your backup plans in the event that a right person leaves a key seat?

One notable distinction between wrong people and right people is that the former see themselves as having "jobs," while the latter see themselves as having *responsibilities*. Every person in a key seat should be able to respond to the question "What do you do?" *not* with a job title, but with a statement of personal responsibility. "I'm the one person ultimately responsible for *x* and *y*. When I look to the left, to the right, in front, in back, there is no one ultimately responsible but me. And I accept that responsibility." When executive teams visit our research laboratory, I sometimes begin by challenging them to introduce themselves not by using their titles, but by articulating their responsibilities. Some find this to be easy, but those who have lost (or not yet built) a culture of discipline find this question to be terribly difficult.

As Bank of America rose to greatness, the responsibility for sound loan decisions lay squarely on the shoulders of loan managers distributed across California; the loan manager in Modesto or Stockton or Anaheim had nowhere to look but in the mirror to assign responsibility for the quality of his or her loan portfolio. As Bank of America began to fall, however, a complex layering of about one hundred loan committees and as many as fifteen required signatures subverted the concept of responsibility. Who is the one person responsible for a loan decision? If I've put the loan request through a dozen committees and obtained fifteen signatures, then it can't possibly be *my* fault if it turns out to be a bad loan. Someone else—the system!—is responsible. Mediocre loan officers could hide behind the bureaucracy, while self-disciplined officers found themselves increasingly frustrated by a system designed to compensate for incompetent colleagues. "One of the great tragedies of this company," commented a Bank of America executive at the time, "is that it lost a lot of good young people because we weren't a meritocracy." [72]

Throughout our research studies, we found that dramatic leaps in performance came when an executive team of exceptional leaders coalesced and made a series of outstanding, supremely well-executed decisions. Whether a company sustains exceptional performance depends first and foremost on whether it continues to have the right people in power, which brings us to the last point in this stage.

PROBLEMATIC SUCCESSION OF POWER

On March 15, 44 BC, Gaius Julius Caesar bled to death in Pompeii's Theatre of Rome, punctured by twenty-three stab wounds. In his will, Caesar had adopted and named as his heir his grandnephew, Octavian. Only eighteen years old at the time, Octavian first appeared to be a marginal player compared to

Caesar's longtime allies Mark Antony and Cleopatra (the mother of Caesar's biological son), and of little threat to Caesar's enemies. But Octavian proved a shrewd student of power, assembling legions of Julius Caesar's loyal soldiers into a private army and demolishing Caesar's enemies in 42 BC before facing off against Antony and Cleopatra. Meanwhile, Octavian legitimized his power in the eyes of the Senate, deftly refusing honors that might have appeared contrary to Roman tradition and accepting only powers—often with feigned protestations—granted by the Senate. Step by step over the course of two decades, Octavian transformed himself into the first emperor of Rome, known to history as Augustus. He ruled the Empire for more than four decades.

In his wonderful course "Emperors of Rome," Professor Garrett G. Fagan shows Augustus to be one of the most effective statesmen in history. He unified Rome, eliminating the civil wars that had ripped apart the Republic.[73] He redesigned the system of government, brought peace, expanded the Empire, and increased prosperity. He avoided ostentation, living in a relatively modest house, and displayed a peculiar genius for political maneuvering, achieving objectives largely by making "suggestions" rather than invoking formal legal or military power.

But Augustus failed to solve a chronic problem that significantly hurt the Empire over the subsequent centuries: succession. After Augustus, Rome ping-ponged between competent leaders and despotic, even semi-deranged, titans like Caligula and Nero. And while the fall of the Roman Empire cannot be explained entirely by problematic successions of power, Augustus failed to create effective mechanisms that would produce an effective transfer of power to generations of outstanding leadership.

> Leaders who fail the process of succession set their enterprises on a path to decline. Sometimes they wait too long; sometimes they never address the question at all; sometimes they have bad luck and their chosen successor leaves or dies; sometimes they deliberately set their successor up for failure; and sometimes they just flat out pick badly. But however and whenever it happens, one of the most significant indicators of decline is the reallocation of power into the hands of leaders who fail to comprehend and/or lack the will to do what must be done—and equally, what must *not* be done—to sustain greatness.

In all but one case in our analysis of decline (the one exception being Circuit City), we observed signs of a problematic succession of power by the end of Stage 2. We observed each of the following modes of turmoil in at least one of the fallen companies:

- A domineering leader fails to develop strong successors (or drives strong successors away) and thereby creates a leadership vacuum when he or she steps away.
- An able executive dies or departs unexpectedly, with no strong replacement to step smoothly into the role.
- Strong successor candidates turn down the opportunity to become CEO.

- Strong successor candidates unexpectedly leave the company.
- The board of directors is acrimoniously divided on the designation of a leader, creating an adversarial "we" and "they" dynamic at the top.
- Leaders stay in power as long as they can and then pass the company to leaders who are late in their careers and assume a caretaker role.
- Monarchy-style family dynamics favor family members over non-family members, regardless of who would be the best leader.
- The board brings in a leader from the outside who doesn't fit the core values, and the leader is ejected by the culture like a virus.
- The company chronically fails at getting CEO selection right.

From what we've seen in this study, Stage 2 overreaching tends to increase after a legendary leader steps away. Perhaps those who assume power next feel extra pressure to be bold, visionary, and aggressive, to live up to the implicit expectations of their predecessor or the irrational expectations of Wall Street, which accentuates Stage 2. Or perhaps legendary leaders pick successors less capable in a subconscious (or maybe even conscious) strategy to increase their own status by comparison. But whatever the underlying dynamic, when companies engage in Stage 2 overreaching *and* bungle the transfer of power, they tend to hurtle downward toward Stage 3 and beyond.

Over the years of conducting my research, I've been a leadership skeptic, influenced by the evidence that complex organizations achieve greatness through the efforts of more than one exceptional individual. The best leaders we've studied had a peculiar genius for seeing themselves as not all that important, recognizing the need to build an executive team and to craft a culture based on core values that do not depend upon a single heroic leader. But in cases of decline, we find a more pronounced role for the powerful individual, and not for the better. So, even though I remain a leadership skeptic, the evidence leads me to this sobering conclusion: while no leader can single-handedly build an enduring great company, the wrong leader vested with power can almost single-handedly bring a company down.

Choose well.

MARKERS FOR STAGE 2

• **UNSUSTAINABLE QUEST FOR GROWTH, CONFUSING BIG WITH GREAT:** Success creates pressure for more growth, setting up a vicious cycle of expectations; this strains people, the culture, and systems to the breaking point; unable to deliver consistent tactical excellence, the institution frays at the edges.

• **UNDISCIPLINED DISCONTINUOUS LEAPS:** The enterprise makes dramatic moves that fail at least one of the following three tests: 1. Do they ignite passion and fit with the company's core values? 2. Can the organization be the best in the world at these activities or in these arenas? 3. Will these activities help drive the organization's economic or resource engine?

• **DECLINING PROPORTION OF RIGHT PEOPLE IN KEY SEATS:** There is a declining proportion of right people in key seats, because of losing the right people and/or growing beyond the organization's ability to get enough people to execute on that growth with excellence (e.g., breaking Packard's Law).

• **EASY CASH ERODES COST DISCIPLINE:** The organization responds to increasing costs by increasing prices and revenues rather than increasing discipline.

• **BUREAUCRACY SUBVERTS DISCIPLINE:** A system of bureaucratic rules subverts the ethic of freedom and responsibility that marks a culture of discipline; people increasingly think in terms of "jobs" rather than *responsibilities*.

• **PROBLEMATIC SUCCESSION OF POWER:** The organization experiences leadership-transition difficulties, be they in the form of poor succession planning, failure to groom excellent leaders from within, political turmoil, bad luck, or an unwise selection of successors.

- **PERSONAL INTERESTS PLACED ABOVE ORGANIZATIONAL INTERESTS:** People in power allocate more for themselves or their constituents—more money, more privileges, more fame, more of the spoils of success—seeking to capitalize as much as possible in the short term, rather than investing primarily in building for greatness decades into the future.

STAGE 3:
DENIAL OF RISK AND PERIL

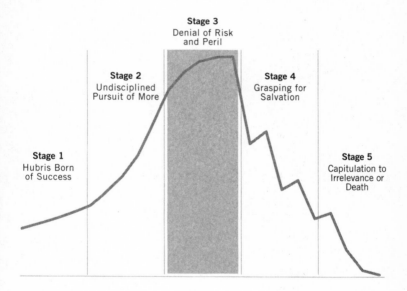

Stage 3
Denial of Risk
and Peril

Stage 2
Undisciplined
Pursuit of More

Stage 4
Grasping for
Salvation

Stage 1
Hubris Born
of Success

Stage 5
Capitulation to
Irrelevance or
Death

In 1985, a Motorola engineer vacationed in the Bahamas. His wife tried to keep in touch with her clients via cell phone (which had only recently been offered to consumers for the first time) but found herself stymied. This sparked an idea: why not create a grid of satellites that could ensure a crisp phone connection from any point on Earth? You may remember reading how New

Zealand mountaineer Rob Hall died on Mount Everest in 1996 and how he bade farewell to his wife thousands of miles away as his life ebbed away in the cold at 28,000 feet. His parting words— "Sleep well, my sweetheart. Please don't worry too much"— riveted the world's attention. Without a satellite phone link, Hall would not have been able to have that last conversation with his life partner. Motorola envisioned making this type of anywhere-on-Earth connection available to people everywhere with its bold venture called Iridium.[74]

Motorola's second-generation chief executive Robert Galvin had assiduously avoided big discontinuous leaps, favoring instead a series of well-planned, empirically tested evolutionary steps in which new little things turned into new big things that replaced old big things, in a continuous cycle of renewal. Galvin saw Iridium as a small experiment that, if successful, could turn into a Very Big Thing. In the late 1980s, he allocated seed capital to prototype a low-orbiting satellite system. In 1991, Motorola spun out the Iridium project into a separate company, with Motorola as the largest shareholder, and continued to fund concept development. By 1996, Motorola had invested $537 million in the venture and had guaranteed $750 million in loan capacity on Iridium's behalf, the combined amount exceeding Motorola's entire profit for 1996.[75]

In their superb analysis "Learning from Corporate Mistakes: The Rise and Fall of Iridium," Sydney Finkelstein and Shade H. Sanford demonstrate that the pivotal moment for Iridium came in 1996, not at its inception in the 1980s.[76] In the technology-development stage prior to 1996, Iridium could have been suspended with relatively little loss. After that, it entered the launch phase. To go forward would require a greater investment than had been spent for all the development up to that point; after all, you can't launch sixty-six satellites as a cheap experiment.

But by 1996, years after Galvin had retired (and years after he'd allocated seed capital), the case for Iridium had become much less compelling. Traditional cellular service now blanketed much of the globe, erasing much of Iridium's unique value. If the Motorola scientist's wife had tried to call her clients from vacation in 1996, odds are she would have found a good cell connection. Furthermore, the Iridium phones had significant disadvantages. A handset nearly the size of a brick that worked only outside (where you can get a direct ping to a satellite) proved less useful than a traditional cell phone. How many people would lug a brick halfway around the world, only to take the elevator to street level to make an expensive phone call, or ask a cab driver to stop in order to step onto a street corner to check in with the office? Iridium handsets cost $3,000, with calls running at $3 to $7 per minute, while cell phone charges continued to drop. Sure, people in remote places could benefit from Iridium, but remote places lacked the one thing Iridium needed: customers. There just aren't that many people who need to call home from the South Pole or the top of Mount Everest.[77]

When the Motorola engineer came up with the idea for Iridium in 1985, few people envisioned cellular service's nearly ubiquitous coverage. But by 1996, empirical evidence weighed against making the big launch. Meanwhile, Motorola had multiplied revenues fivefold, from $5 billion to $27 billion, fueled by its Stage 2–like commitment to double in size every five years (a goal put in place after Robert Galvin retired).[78] Motorola hoped for a big hit with Iridium, and its 1997 annual report boasted, "With the development of the IRIDIUM® global personal communications system, Motorola has created a new industry."[79] And so, despite the mounting negative evidence, Iridium launched, and in 1998 went live for customers. The very next year Iridium filed for bankruptcy, defaulting on $1.5 billion in loans.[80] Motorola's 1999 proxy report recorded more than $2 billion in charges related to the Iridium program, which helped accelerate Motorola's plummet toward Stage 4.[81]

MAKING BIG BETS IN THE FACE OF MOUNTING EVIDENCE TO THE CONTRARY

As companies move into Stage 3, we begin to see the cumulative effects of the previous stages. Stage 1 hubris leads to Stage 2 overreaching, which sets the company up for Stage 3, Denial of Risk and Peril. This describes what happened with Iridium. In contrast, let's look at Texas Instruments (TI) and its gradual evolution to become the Intel of digital-signal processing, or DSP.

In the late 1970s, TI engineers came up with a great idea to help children learn to spell: an electronic toy that "spoke" words and then asked kids to type the word on a keypad. This was the genesis of Speak & Spell, the first consumer product to use DSP technology. (DSP chips enable analog chunks of data, such as voice, music, and video, to be crunched and reassembled like digital bits.) In 1979, TI made a tiny bet of $150,000 (less than one hundredth of one percent of 1979 revenues) to further investigate DSP, and by 1986, TI had garnered $6 million in revenues from DSP chips—hardly enough to justify a bet-the-company move, but enough evidence to support their continued exploration of DSP. TI customers found new uses for DSP (e.g., modems, speech translation, and communications), and TI set up separate DSP business units.[82] Then in 1993, TI scored a contract to create DSP chips for Nokia's digital cell phones, and by 1997, it had DSP chips in more than twenty-two million phones.

And *that's* when TI set the audacious goal to become the Intel of DSP. "When somebody says DSP," said CEO Tom Engibous, "I want them to think of TI, just like they think of Intel when they say microprocessors."[83] In a bold stroke, he sold both TI's defense and memory-chip businesses, having the guts to *shrink* the company to increase its focus on DSP. By 2004, TI had half of the $8 billion rapidly growing DSP market.[84]

Note that TI dared its big leap only after diligently turning the DSP flywheel for fifteen years. It didn't bet big in 1978, when it had the Speak & Spell. It didn't bet big in 1982, when it first put DSP on a single chip. It didn't bet big in 1986, when it had only $6 million in DSP revenues. Engibous set a big, hairy goal, to be sure, but not one born of hubris or denial of risk. Drawing upon two decades of growing empirical evidence, he set the goal based on a firm foundation of proven success.

The point is not that Motorola erred in its early development of Iridium or that TI had greater prescience in developing DSP. If you always knew ahead of time which new ideas would work for sure, you would invest in only those. But you don't. That's why great companies experiment with a lot of little things that might not pan out in the end. At the start of Iridium and DSP, both Motorola and TI wisely invested in small-scale experimentation and development, but TI, unlike Motorola, bet big only once it had the weight of accumulated empirical evidence on its side. Audacious goals stimulate progress, but big bets without empirical validation, or that fly in the face of mounting evidence, can bring companies down, unless they're blessed with unusual luck. And luck is not a reliable strategy.

Now you might be thinking, "OK, so just don't ignore the evidence—just don't launch an Iridium when the data is so clear—and we'll avoid Stage 3." But life doesn't always present the facts with stark clarity; the situation can be confusing, noisy, unclear, open to interpretation. And in fact, the greatest danger comes not in ignoring clear and unassailable facts, but in misinterpreting *ambiguous* data in situations when you face severe or catastrophic consequences if the ambiguity resolves itself in a way that's not in your favor. To illustrate, I'm going to digress to review the tale of a famous tragedy.

TAKING RISKS BELOW THE WATERLINE

On the afternoon of January 27, 1986, a NASA manager contacted engineers at Morton Thiokol, a subcontractor that provided rocket motors to NASA. The forecast for the Kennedy Space Center in Florida, where the space shuttle *Challenger* sat in preparation for a scheduled launch the next day, called for temperatures in the twenties during early morning hours of the 28th, with the launch-time temperature expected to remain below 30 degrees F. The NASA manager asked the Morton Thiokol engineers to consider the effect of cold weather on the solid-rocket motors, and the engineers quickly assembled to discuss a specific component called an O-ring. When rocket fuel ignites, the rubber-like O-rings seal joints—like putty in a crack—against searing hot gases that, if uncontained, could cause a catastrophic explosion.

The lowest launch temperature in all twenty-four previous shuttle launches had been 53 degrees, more than twenty degrees above the forecast for the next day's scheduled launch, and the engineers had no conclusive data about what would happen to the O-rings at 25 or 30 degrees. They did have some data to suggest that colder temperatures harden O-rings, thereby increasing the time they'd take to seal. (Think of a frozen rubber band in your freezer contrasted with that same rubber band at room temperature and how it becomes much less malleable.) The engineers discussed their initial concerns and scheduled a teleconference with thirty-four people from NASA and Morton Thiokol for 8:15 p.m. Eastern.[85]

The teleconference began with nearly an hour of discussion, leading up to Morton Thiokol's engineering conclusion that it could not recommend launch below 53 degrees. NASA engineers pointed out that the data were conflicting and inconclusive. Yes, the data clearly showed O-ring damage on launches below 60 degrees, but the data *also* showed O-ring damage on a 75-degree launch. "They did have a lot of conflicting data in there," reflected a NASA engineer. "I can't emphasize that enough." Adding further confusion, Morton Thiokol hadn't challenged on previous flights that had projected launch temperatures below 53 degrees (none close to the twenties, to be sure, but lower than the now-stated 53-degree mark), which appeared inconsistent with their current recommendations. And even if the first O-ring were to fail, a redundant second O-ring was supposed to seal into place.

In her authoritative book *The Challenger Launch Decision*, sociologist Diane Vaughan demolishes the myth that NASA managers ignored unassailable data and launched a mission absolutely known to be unsafe. In fact, the conversations on the evening before launch reflected the confusion and shifting views of the participants. At one point, a NASA manager blurted, "My God, Thiokol, when do you want me to launch, next April?" But at another point on the same evening, NASA managers expressed reservations about the launch; a lead NASA engineer pleaded with his people not to let him make a mistake and stated, "I will not agree to launch against the contractor's recommendation." The deliberations lasted for nearly three hours. If the data had been clear, would they have needed a three-hour discussion? Data analyst extraordinaire Edward Tufte shows in his book *Visual Explanations* that if the engineers had plotted the data points in a compelling graphic, they might have seen a clear trend line: *every* launch below 66 degrees showed evidence of

O-ring damage. But no one laid out the data in a clear and convincing visual manner, and the trend toward increased danger in colder temperatures remained obscured throughout the late-night teleconference debate. Summing up, the O-Ring Task Force chair noted, "We just didn't have enough conclusive data to convince anyone."

Convince anyone of *what* exactly? That's the crux of the matter. Somehow, in all the dialogue, the decision frame had turned 180 degrees. Instead of framing the question, "Can you prove that it's *safe* to launch?"—as had traditionally guided launch decisions—the frame inverted to "Can you prove that it's *un*safe to launch?" If they hadn't made that all-important shift or if the data had been absolutely definitive, *Challenger* very likely would have remained on the launch pad until later in the day. After all, the downside of a disaster so totally dwarfed the downside of waiting a few hours that it would be difficult to argue for running such an unbalanced risk. If you're a NASA manager concerned about your career, why would you push for a decision to launch if you saw a very high likelihood it would end in catastrophe? No rational person would do that. But the data were highly ambiguous and the decision criteria had changed. Unable to prove beyond a reasonable doubt that it was *un*safe to launch, Morton Thiokol reversed its stance and voted to launch, faxing its confirmation to NASA shortly before midnight. At 11:38 the next morning, in 36-degree temperatures, an O-ring failed upon ignition, and 73 seconds later, *Challenger* exploded into a fireball. All seven crew members perished as remnants of *Challenger* fell nine miles into the ocean.

The *Challenger* story highlights a key lesson. When facing irreversible decisions that have significant, negative consequences if they go awry—what we might call "launch decisions"—the case for launch should require a preponderance of empirical evidence that it's safe to do so. Had the burden of proof rested on the side of safety ("If we cannot prove beyond a reasonable doubt that it's *safe* to launch, we delay") rather than the other way around, *Challenger* might have been spared its tragedy.

Bill Gore, founder of W. L. Gore & Associates, articulated a helpful concept for decision making and risk taking, what he called the "waterline" principle. Think of being on a ship, and imagine that any decision gone bad will blow a hole in the side of the ship. If you blow a hole above the waterline (where the ship won't take on water and possibly sink), you can patch the hole, learn from the experience, and sail on. But if you blow a hole below the waterline, you can find yourself facing gushers of water pouring in, pulling you toward the ocean floor.[86] And if it's a big enough hole, you might go down really fast, just like some of the financial-company catastrophes in 2008.

To be clear, great enterprises *do* make big bets, but they avoid big bets that could blow holes below the waterline. When making risky bets and decisions in the face of ambiguous or conflicting data, ask three questions:

1. What's the upside, if events turn out well?
2. What's the downside, if events go very badly?
3. Can you live with the downside? Truly?

Suppose you are on the side of a cliff with a potential storm bearing down, but you don't know for sure how bad the storm will be or whether it will involve dangerous lightning. You have to decide: do we go up, or do we go down? Two climbers in Eldorado Canyon, Colorado, faced this scenario on a famous climb called the Naked Edge. A Colorado summer storm roiled in the distance, and they had to decide whether to continue with their planned outing for the day. Now think of the three questions. What's the upside if the storm passes by uneventfully? They complete their planned ascent for the day. What's the downside if the storm turns into a full-fledged fusillade of lightning while they're sitting high on the exposed summit pitch? They can die. They chose to continue. They anchored into the top of the cliff, perched right out on the top of an exposed pinnacle, just as the storm rushed into the canyon. The ropes popped and buzzed with building electricity. Then—bang!—a lightning bolt hit the top climber, melting his metal gear and killing him instantly.[87]

Of course, probabilities play a role in this thinking. If the probability of events going terribly awry is, for all practical purposes, zero, or if it is small but stable, that leads to different decisions than if the probability is high, increasing, unstable, or highly ambiguous. (Otherwise, we would never get on a commercial airliner, never mind climb the Naked Edge or El Capitan.) The climbers on the Naked Edge saw increasing probability of a bad storm in an asymmetric-risk scenario (minimal upside with catastrophic downside) yet went ahead anyway.

The 2008 financial crisis underscores how mismanaging these questions can destroy companies. As the housing market bubble grew, so did the probability of a real estate crash. What's the upside of increasing leverage dramatically (in some cases 30 to 1, or more) and increasing exposure to mortgage-backed securities? More profit, if the weather remains clear and calm. What's the downside if the entire housing market crashes and we enter one of the most perilous credit crises in history? Merrill Lynch sells out its independence to Bank of America. Fannie Mae gets taken over by the government. Bear Stearns flails and then disappears in a takeover. And Lehman Brothers fails outright, sending the financial markets into a liquidity crisis that sends the economy spiraling downward.

A CULTURE OF DENIAL

Of course, not every case of decline involves big launch decisions like Iridium, or lethal decisions like going for the summit on a dangerous rock climb. Companies can also *gradually* weaken, and as they move deeper into Stage 3, they begin to accumulate warning signs. They might see a decline in customer engagement, an erosion of inventory turns, a subtle decline in margins, a loss in pricing power, or any number of other indicators of growing mediocrity. What indicators should you most closely track? For businesses, our analysis suggests that any deterioration in gross margins, current ratio, or debt-to-equity ratio indicates an impending storm. Our financial analyses revealed that all eleven fallen companies showed a negative trend in at least one of these three variables as they moved toward Stage 4, yet we found little evidence of significant management concern and certainly not the productive paranoia they should have had about these trends. Customer loyalty and stakeholder engagement also deserve attention. And as we discussed in Stage 2, take heed of any decline in the proportion of right people in key seats.

As companies hurtle deeper into Stage 3, the inner workings of the leadership team can veer away from the behaviors we found on teams that built great companies. In the table "Leadership-Team Dynamics," I've contrasted the leadership dynamics of companies on the way down with companies on the way up.

LEADERSHIP-TEAM DYNAMICS:
ON THE WAY DOWN VERSUS ON THE WAY UP

Teams on the Way Down	Teams on the Way Up
People shield those in power from grim facts, fearful of penalty and criticism for shining light on the harsh realities.	People bring forth unpleasant facts—"Come here, look, man, this is *ugly*"—to be discussed; leaders never criticize those who bring forth harsh realities.
People assert strong opinions without providing data, evidence, or a solid argument.	People bring data, evidence, logic, and solid arguments to the discussion.
The team leader has a very low questions-to-statements ratio, avoiding critical input and/or allowing sloppy reasoning and unsupported opinions.	The team leader employs a Socratic style, using a high questions-to-statements ratio, challenging people, and pushing for penetrating insight.
Team members acquiesce to a decision yet do not unify to make the decision successful, or worse, undermine the decision after the fact.	Team members unify behind a decision once made and work to make the decision succeed, even if they vigorously disagreed with the decision.
Team members seek as much credit as possible for themselves yet do not enjoy the confidence and admiration of their peers.	Each team member credits other people for success yet enjoys the confidence and admiration of his or her peers.
Team members argue to look smart or to improve their own interests rather than argue to find the best answers to support the overall cause.	Team members argue and debate, not to improve their personal position, but to find the best answers to support the overall cause.

| The team conducts "autopsies with blame," seeking culprits rather than wisdom. | The team conducts "autopsies without blame," mining wisdom from painful experiences. |
| Team members often fail to deliver exceptional results, and blame other people or outside factors for setbacks, mistakes, and failures. | Each team member delivers exceptional results, yet in the event of a setback, each accepts full responsibility and learns from mistakes. |

One common behavior of late Stage 3 (and that often carries well into Stage 4) is when those in power blame other people or external factors—or otherwise explain away the data—rather than confront the frightening reality that the enterprise may be in serious trouble. As IBM began its historic fall in the late 1980s and early 1990s, it faced the onslaught of distributed computing that threatened its mainframe business. An executive who reported these disturbing trends to IBM senior leadership found himself chastised, a powerful IBM leader brushing his report aside with a dismissive sweep of the hand: "There must be something wrong with your data." The young executive knew then IBM would fall. "Doing a start-up seemed less risky than working in a climate of denial," he later quipped about his decision to leave IBM to become an entrepreneur. IBM reorganized and re-engineered, but it didn't successfully address the perilous erosion of its position until it had fallen so far that it would be likened in 1992 to a dinosaur, soon to be extinct. In his historic turnaround of IBM (which we will discuss in subsequent pages), Louis V. Gerstner, Jr. confronted the harsh reality of IBM's shortcomings head-on, challenging his team early in his tenure, "One hundred and twenty-five thousand IBMers are gone . . . Who did it to them? Was it an act of God? These guys came in and beat us." [88]

In this analysis, we found evidence of externalizing blame during the era of decline in seven of eleven cases. When Zenith hit a hard patch in the mid-1970s, its CEO pointed out the window to a range of factors: "Who could have predicted the Arabs could have gotten together on *any* subject? Who could have foreseen Watergate? The great inflation we had? . . . Then we were hit by a strike."[89] Zenith also began to blame "unfair" Japanese competition for eroding profits and declining market share. Even if the Japanese did compete unfairly (although the Justice Department did not act in response to Zenith's pleas for help), Zenith's response to the Japanese resembled that of the American auto industry in the same era, a failure to confront head-on the fact that the Japanese had learned how to lower costs *and* increase quality. Shortly thereafter, Zenith fell into Stage 4.

One final manifestation of denial deserves special attention: obsessive reorganization. By 1961, Scott Paper had built the most successful paper-based consumer products franchise in the world, with commanding positions in all manner of products, including napkins, towels, and tissue. Then P&G entered Scott's territory for the first time, while other companies like Kimberly-Clark and Georgia Pacific persistently encroached on Scott's markets. P&G launched Bounty paper towels on the high end, while private label brands encircled Scott from below. From 1960 to 1971, Scott's share of the paper-based consumer business fell from nearly half the market to a third.[90] Then in 1971, P&G went national with its Charmin toilet tissue—a direct assault on one of Scott's most important product lines.

And how did Scott respond?

By reorganizing.[91]

Scott restructured marketing and research, moving boxes around on the organizational chart, but failed to mount a vigorous response to Charmin for five years.[92] Five years! Scott continued to restructure through the 1980s, at one point reorganizing three times in four years.[93] With eroding market share in nearly every category, Scott Paper fell into Stage 4.[94]

> Reorganizations and restructurings can create a false sense that you're actually *doing* something productive. Companies are in the process of reorganizing themselves all the time; that's the nature of institutional evolution. But when you begin to respond to data and warning signs with reorganization as a primary strategy, you may well be in denial. It's a bit like responding to a severe heart condition or a cancer diagnosis by rearranging your living room.

There is no organizational utopia. All organizational structures have trade-offs, and every type of organization has inefficiencies. We have no evidence from our research that any one structure is ideal in all situations, and no form of reorganization can make risk and peril melt away.

MARKERS FOR STAGE 3

- **AMPLIFY THE POSITIVE, DISCOUNT THE NEGATIVE:** There is a tendency to discount or explain away negative data rather than presume that something is wrong with the company; leaders highlight and amplify external praise and publicity.

- **BIG BETS AND BOLD GOALS WITHOUT EMPIRICAL VALIDATION:** Leaders set audacious goals and/or make big bets that aren't based on accumulated experience, or worse, that fly in the face of the facts.

- **INCURRING HUGE DOWNSIDE RISK BASED ON AMBIGUOUS DATA:** When faced with ambiguous data and decisions that have a potentially severe or catastrophic downside, leaders take a positive view of the data and run the risk of blowing a hole "below the waterline."

- **EROSION OF HEALTHY TEAM DYNAMICS:** There is a marked decline in the quality and amount of dialogue and debate; there is a shift toward either consensus or dictatorial management rather than a process of argument and disagreement followed by unified commitment to execute decisions.

- **EXTERNALIZING BLAME:** Rather than accept full responsibility for setbacks and failures, leaders point to external factors or other people to affix blame.

- **OBSESSIVE REORGANIZATIONS:** Rather than confront the brutal realities, the enterprise chronically reorganizes; people are increasingly preoccupied with internal politics rather than external conditions.

- **IMPERIOUS DETACHMENT:** Those in power become more imperious and detached; symbols and perks of executive-class status amplify detachment; plush new office buildings may disconnect executives from daily life.

STAGE 4:
GRASPING FOR SALVATION

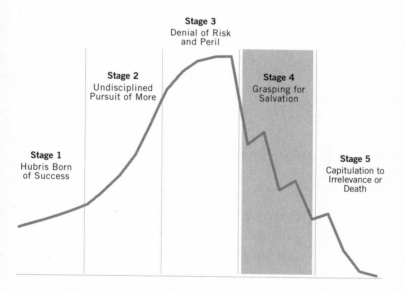

Stage 3
Denial of Risk
and Peril

Stage 2
Undisciplined
Pursuit of More

Stage 4
Grasping for
Salvation

Stage 1
Hubris Born
of Success

Stage 5
Capitulation to
Irrelevance or
Death

From 1992 through 1998, HP's CEO Lew Platt led his company to quintuple profits and multiply cumulative stock returns by more than five times, a performance that would make Platt #11 on a ranking of wealth creators over a twenty-five-year period according to *Chief Executive* magazine. Yet by early 1999, Platt would be regarded by many—investors, analysts, the business media—as struggling, perhaps even failing, as HP tried to get its bearings in the new Internet economy.[95]

While I do not share the assessment of Platt as a failure, he did make one misstep that set HP and himself up for a fall: trying to grow an increasingly large company at an unsustainable rate. It had taken HP more than half a century to reach $15 billion in annual revenues; under Platt, it took only four years to break $30 billion and only three additional years to surpass $45 billion. Unable to sustain its torrid growth rate, HP hit a wall in 1998 and disappointed Wall Street for five quarters. If Platt had left some growth on the table, thereby making it easier to maintain a smooth growth trajectory, HP might have soared right through the late 1990s as a success story. Instead, Platt was out of a job.[96]

In January 1999, HP's board of directors gathered at the Garden Court Hotel in Palo Alto, California. Two well-written chronicles of this era, *Backfire* by Peter Burrows and *Perfect Enough* by George Anders, describe the meeting as a pivotal moment. HP employees had watched first with befuddlement then amazement then fear as the Great Internet Bubble of the late 1990s distorted the laws of economics. By 1999, Internet companies like Amazon and Yahoo! had zoomed from zero to more than $15 billion in market capitalization in five years—a feat that'd taken HP more than ten times as long.[97]

Whereas Platt, with his thick glasses, penchant for driving plain-vanilla Ford Taurus cars, and humble eat-in-the-lunch-room-with-employees demeanor, might have been ideal for an earlier era, HP's stalling growth and languishing stock price (relative to the skyrocketing technology sector) lent credence to a growing worry that HP needed an entirely new type of leader. And so the fifty-seven-year-old Platt suggested that perhaps he should step aside early and give the keys to the next generation. The board accepted his resignation and launched a search for HP's next CEO.[98]

On July 19, 1999, HP announced Platt's replacement, Carly Fiorina from Lucent Technologies. In 1998, *Fortune* had named this "supersaleswoman" the #1 "Most Powerful Woman in Business," beating out Oprah Winfrey for the top spot.[99] The announcement that staid, old HP had hired the most powerful, glamorous, exciting, magnetic, superstar female executive in the world ignited a frenzy that stunned even Fiorina. Not only did *Forbes, Fortune,* and *Business Week* want a slice of the story, but so did Big Media like *The Oprah Winfrey Show,* Diane Sawyer, *Glamour,* and *Vogue.* To Fiorina's credit, she did not accept all the invitations, turning down some of the most high-profile ones.[100] Still, the calls poured in and HP found itself with a celebrity CEO, a business rock star who could charm and dazzle and whose very presence created a media onslaught. Within forty-eight hours of becoming CEO, Fiorina attracted attention at prominent outlets like the *Wall Street Journal, CNBC,* the *Washington Post,* and the *New York Times.* Within two weeks, *Business Week* featured her in a cover story.[101]

Quite a contrast to Louis V. Gerstner, Jr., the CEO brought in to lead IBM (HP's success contrast in this analysis) during its dark days in 1993. When *USA Today* offered to publicize a "daily progress chart" as Gerstner moved through his first 100 days, he replied, "No, thank you. We're going dark for a bit while we assess the task at hand."[102] Instead of going to headquarters on his first day, he chose to visit an international managers' meeting. But Gerstner didn't have an IBM security badge yet, and he found himself stranded and forlorn outside a locked, imposing office building. "There I was, the new CEO, knocking helplessly on the door, hoping to draw someone's attention to let me in," Gerstner wrote in his wonderful book *Who Says Elephants Can't Dance?* "After a while a cleaning woman arrived, checked me out rather skeptically, then opened the door—I suspect more to stop my pounding on the door than from any sense on her part that I belonged on the inside rather than the outside of the building. I wandered around and eventually found the conference room where the meeting was just about to begin." [103]

Shortly into her tenure, Fiorina starred in a television commercial, standing in front of the fabled Palo Alto garage where Hewlett and Packard started their company in the late 1930s. "The company of Bill Hewlett and Dave Packard is being reinvented," she beautifully articulated. "The original start-up will act like one again. Watch!" [104] In conjunction with an army of fellow "change warriors," Fiorina led a dramatic and inspiring transformation, motivating the troops with her soaring message. [105] She set grand, sweeping strategies, unifying HP's brand under the slogan "Invent," creating marketing sizzle, and galvanizing HP people to move at Net Speed. *Forbes* ran a cover story titled "The Cult of Carly," the opening page of the article blaring in a font size that filled nearly half a page, "All Carly, All the Time," and quoting Fiorina later in the article that "Leadership is a performance." [106] Fiorina gave a rousing speech to a packed gathering of HP faithful, "We owe you a very clear vision of the future . . . and that's what we intend to give you." [107]

Gerstner took a very different approach, stating at his first public discussion about IBM, "The last thing IBM needs right now is a vision." By this, Gerstner did not mean that IBM shouldn't ever have a vision, but that his first priorities lay in more basic activities: making sure he had the right people in key seats ("my top priority during those first few weeks"), regaining profitability, increasing cash flow, and above all, putting the customer back at the center of everything IBM did.[108] Gerstner took a pedestrian approach, building on existing strengths and working with "massive amounts of quantitative analysis."[109] He took nearly three months to thoroughly understand IBM's situation. "It would not be believable that after 30 days somebody could lay out a timetable for changing a company of this size," Gerstner told *Fortune* editor David Kirkpatrick. "Besides, I really do want to disabuse your readers of the concept that there's going to be this grand plan that's going to emerge from the new management at some point. It isn't going to happen."

At the end of Gerstner's first 100 days, *USA Today* ran a cover story highlighting the fact that IBM stock had declined 6 percent since he became CEO, in large part because, in the words of one critical analyst, "He's done nothing." Another summed up, "Clearly, he is not a miracle worker." When asked about the sense of crisis at IBM, Gerstner responded tersely, "I don't have a sense of crisis. I have a sense of urgency that never changes, whether we're doing well or we're doing poorly . . . But by no means do I think this company is in crisis."[110]

Gerstner's self-imposed discipline to get the right people in place first, then proceed to understand IBM's situation, and only then to settle upon a vision and strategy contrasted with Fiorina's approach. In a *Business Week* interview conducted within one day of HP's announcement of her as CEO, Fiorina mapped out her priorities, with Job One being to craft a vision for HP as an Internet company that could stitch together a vast range of products.[111] "I had come into HP with a belief that we were running

out of time," Fiorina later wrote in her memoir, *Tough Choices*.
"I was in a hurry . . ."[112] Gerstner and Fiorina also contrasted
with each other where it most matters: results. Gerstner steadily
increased profitability; Fiorina did not. IBM's return on sales
grew smoothly during Gerstner's tenure, starting at 5 percent
during his first full year and reaching 9 percent during his final
full year at Big Blue. In contrast, HP's return on sales showed a
much more erratic pattern, starting at 7 percent during Fiorina's
first full year, turning negative in 2002 with HP's first annual
loss in its 45-year history as a public company (due in large part
to restructuring and other charges related to a major acquisition), and ending at 4 percent during her last full year at HP.

Fiorina's tenure came to an end on February 7, 2005, when
the HP board met in special session at the Chicago airport.
Asked to leave the meeting after a short presentation, Fiorina
waited in her hotel room for three hours before being called
back to the conference room. "When I opened the door and realized all but two Board members had already left," she later
wrote, "I knew I had been fired."[113]

SEARCHING FOR A SILVER BULLET

That Fiorina's tenure at HP ended in disappointment cannot be
blamed entirely on her. In fact, Fiorina was exactly what the
board appears to have wanted: a charismatic, visionary leader
who would bring the magnetic star power and passion for
change needed to revolutionize the company. By that standard,
Fiorina can be judged a success, indeed, the perfect choice. The
descent into Stage 4 didn't begin with HP's slow response to the

dot-com bubble or its falling below Wall Street expectations, but in how the board *reacted* to falling behind.

Stage 4 begins when an organization reacts to a downturn by lurching for a silver bullet. This can take a wide range of possible forms, such as betting big on an unproven technology, pinning hopes on an untested strategy, relying upon the success of a splashy new product, seeking a "game changing" acquisition, gambling on an image makeover, hiring consultants who promise salvation, seeking a savior CEO, expounding the rhetoric of "revolution," or in its very late stages, grasping for a financial rescue or buyout. The key point is that they go for a quick, big solution or bold stroke to jump-start a recovery, rather than embark on the more pedestrian, arduous process of rebuilding long-term momentum. The HP board, for instance, continued to exemplify Stage 4 behavior in how it argued for the controversial $24 billion merger with Compaq Computer Corporation in 2002, with dramatic, we-can-change-everything-with-one-big-sweeping-action rhetoric: the "best and fastest way to increase the value" . . . "in one move, we dramatically improve" . . . "we immediately double" . . . "enable us to quickly address" . . . "in a single strategic move" . . . "will allow HP to accelerate" . . . "will transform our industry" . . . and so on.[114] The table below contrasts the behaviors that exemplify and perpetuate Stage 4 with the behaviors that can help reverse the downward spiral.

Behaviors That Exemplify and Perpetuate Stage 4	Behaviors That Can Help Reverse the Downward Spiral of Stage 4
Pin hopes on unproven strategies—discontinuous leaps into new technologies, new markets, new businesses—often with much hype and fanfare.	Formulate strategic changes based on empirical evidence, and extensive strategic and quantitative analysis, rather than make bold, untested leaps.
Seek a big, "game changing" acquisition (often based on hoped-for, but as yet unproven, "synergies") to transform the company in a single stroke.	Understand that combining two struggling companies never makes one great company; only consider strategic acquisitions that amplify proven strengths.
Make panicky, desperate moves in reaction to threats that can imperil the company even more, draining cash and further eroding financial strength.	Get the facts, think, and then act (or not) with calm determination; never take actions that will imperil the company long-term.
Embark on a program of radical change, a revolution, to transform or upend nearly every aspect of the company, jeopardizing or abandoning core strengths.	Gain clarity about what is core and should be held firm, and what needs to change, building upon proven strengths and eliminating weaknesses.
Sell people on the promises of a brighter future to compensate for poor results.	Focus on performance, letting tangible results provide the strongest case for a new direction.
Destroy momentum with chronic restructuring and/or a series of inconsistent big decisions.	Create momentum with a series of good decisions, supremely well executed, that build one upon another.
Search for a leader-as-savior, with a bias for selecting a visionary from the outside who'll ride in and galvanize the company.	Search for a disciplined executive, with a bias for selecting a proven performer from the inside.

Every company in this study that fell into the late stages of decline grasped for at least one silver bullet. (See Appendix 4.B for an evidence table.) For example, Circuit City replaced its retiring homegrown CEO with an executive from Best Buy who had been with Circuit City just eighteen months. Then Circuit City fired more than 3,000 of its highest-paid, more-experienced store employees. Within two years, Circuit City hired Goldman Sachs, pinning hopes on a buyout, only to see a bid from Blockbuster evaporate.[115] Shortly thereafter, Circuit City filed for bankruptcy. Or consider Scott Paper, which vested hope in expensive strategy consultants and fomented a cultural transformation that *Fortune* described as "get religion or get shown the door."[116] Ames hired CEOs, jettisoned CEOs, and hired new CEOs, at one point churning through three management teams in thirty-three months—lurching from strategy to strategy, program to program, looking for a fundamental transformation.[117] Shaken out of its torpor by fierce new competitors, A&P converted more than four thousand stores to a format called WEO (short for "Where Economy Originates"), driving down prices to regain market share in a desperation move described by one industry observer as "a Kamikaze dive." The move proved catastrophic to profitability. A&P abandoned the strategy and hired a charismatic savior from the outside who produced a brief return to profitability, only to resign when A&P collapsed yet again into a string of losses.[118]

Stage 4 grasping can produce a brief improvement, but the results do not last. Dashed hope follows dashed hope follows dashed hope yet again. Companies stuck in Stage 4 try all sorts of new programs, new fads, new strategies, new visions, new cultures, new values, new breakthroughs, new acquisitions, and new saviors. And when one silver bullet fails, they search for another and then yet another. The signature of mediocrity is not an unwillingness to change. The signature of mediocrity is chronic inconsistency.

You might be thinking, "Perhaps grasping for salvation is the rational answer for companies in trouble; dying companies must do desperate things because they're dying." But companies don't generally find themselves on the verge of death at the start of Stage 4. The companies we studied had taken a tumble at the start of Stage 4, to be sure, but not a lethal one. Indeed, by succumbing to Stage 4 behavior, they *worsened* their position, increasing the likelihood that they would become a dying company forced into taking desperate action.

Compare Motorola and TI, two great companies that stumbled; one fell through Stage 4 while the other did not. In 1998, Motorola lost money for the first time in more than fifty years. Top executives sealed themselves off in a conference room, writing ideas on a whiteboard, searching for a breakthrough. They decided upon a path of radical change, what *Business Week* labeled "Shock Therapy." [119] Motorola bought General Instruments Corporation for $17 billion, an amount comparable to Motorola's entire stockholders' equity.[120] It jumped headlong into the Internet and broadband frenzy just before the bubble burst with a strategy called "Intelligence Everywhere." At first, these moves seemed to work, as Motorola's cumulative value to investors more than tripled in two years.[121] Then the Internet and broadband bubbles burst, and Motorola acknowledged in its own 2001 annual report, "Like others, we inopportunely chased the dotcom and telecom boom in 2000." The company had built up manufacturing capacity and a global cost structure to support a $45 billion revenue company going into 2001, but 2001 revenues crashed to $30 billion, and Motorola posted a series of losses.[122] In late 2003, the board selected an outside leader for the first time in the company's history, hiring high-profile Ed Zander from Sun Microsystems; he stepped down four years later, hounded by dissident shareholders.[123]

TI, the success contrast to Motorola, took a completely different approach. TI had been one of the star technology companies of the mid-twentieth century, but it fell from greatness in the 1970s and early 1980s, when it diverged into money-losing consumer businesses such as digital watches and home computers. The board turned to Jerry Junkins in 1985. Unassuming and determined—described by one journalist as "sort of a Texan Jimmy Stewart"—Junkins stepped quietly into the CEO role after working at the company for more than a quarter of a century.[124] He led the first phase of TI's return to greatness by igniting vigorous dialogue and debate, and channeling its efforts into businesses in which it had a chance to become best, a process that ultimately led to the tremendous success of DSP chips that we discussed in Stage 3.[125]

> The leaders at TI understood that rebuilding greatness requires a series of intelligent, well-executed actions that add up one on top of another. Some decisions are bigger than others, but even the biggest decisions account for only a small fraction of the total outcome that makes a great company. Most "overnight success" stories are about twenty years in the making.

On May 29, 1996, Junkins died from heart failure while on a business trip to Europe. The unexpected death of a beloved CEO could throw a company into turmoil, but Tom Engibous, then head of TI's semiconductor division, had been well prepared to assume chief-executive responsibility. With two decades of up-through-the-ranks experience at TI, Engibous became TI's second unassuming, self-deflecting, intensely driven CEO in a row. "Hopefully, this story will focus on TI and not too much on me," he'd admonish those who sought to profile his management style. The company's success "won't be due to his charismatic leadership," wrote Elisa Williams in a *Forbes* article. "Engibous has a personality that's about as nondescript as the midwestern plains he grew up on." [126] At the end of his tenure, Engibous engineered a smooth transition to yet another home-grown leader, Richard Templeton, who'd worked his entire twenty-four years deep inside TI.[127] At the very time that Motorola was falling from good to worse, TI's quiet, determined leaders orchestrated an almost textbook transition, and achieved stock performance five times greater than Motorola's and nearly equal to Intel's from 1995 to 2005.[128]

Our research across multiple studies (*Good to Great, Built to*

Last, How the Mighty Fall, and our ongoing research into what it takes to prevail in turbulent environments) shows a distinct negative correlation between building great companies and going outside for a CEO. Eight of the eleven fallen companies in this analysis went for an outside CEO during their era of decline, whereas only one of the success contrasts went outside during the eras of comparison. Now you might be thinking, "But wouldn't companies in trouble need to go outside?" Perhaps, but keep in mind, in this analysis of decline, performance generally *worsened* under saviors from the outside. And in our previous research, over 90 percent of the CEOs that led companies from good to great came from inside; meanwhile, over two-thirds of the comparison companies in that study hired a CEO from the outside yet failed to make a comparable leap.

How then do we make sense of the IBM case? After all, while IBM brought Gerstner in from RJR Nabisco, the company nonetheless rebounded. (For a summary of IBM's comeback, see Appendix 6.A.) Clearly, an outsider *can* succeed in turning around a company and resetting it on the path to greatness. So, what's the difference between this case and the others? Part of the answer lies in the fact that Gerstner returned to the intense, methodical, and consistent approach that produces greatness in the first place. Gerstner understood that whether you're brought in from the outside or come from the inside, you have to halt the cycle of grasping and cease jumping from one false salvation to another, from silver bullet to silver bullet, from dashed hope to new hope, only to have hopes dashed yet again. When an organization in trouble goes for an outsider, it usually has a tenor of "Help! We need a radical, revolutionary change agent to come in and change *everything*—and *fast*!" If the leader buys into this, he or she is likely to perpetuate Stage 4, not reverse it. The remarkable thing about Gerstner is that he did not accept that frame, a powerful lesson for all leaders, whether coming from within or without.

PANIC AND DESPERATION

When I was fourteen years old, I found myself utterly terrified looking down a 100-foot sheer overhanging rock face while learning to rappel as part of a rock-climbing course. The anchor gear unexpectedly shifted, and I instinctively lurched to grab the lip of the overhang and let go of my rappel brake hand (the hand you keep on the rope to control your descent). By reacting in fear and trying to "save myself," I'd actually increased the danger. Fortunately, my instructor caught me on a backup safety rope, but an important life lesson has stuck with me ever since.

> When we find ourselves in trouble, when we find ourselves on the cusp of falling, our survival instinct—and our fear—can evoke lurching, reactive behavior absolutely contrary to survival. The very moment when we need to take calm, deliberate action, we run the risk of doing the exact opposite and bringing about the very outcomes we most fear.

In looking at companies in decline, I'm struck by this lesson again: by grasping about in fearful, frantic reaction, late Stage 4 companies accelerate their own demise. Of course, their leaders can later claim, "But look at everything we did. We changed everything. We tried everything we could think of. We fired every shot we had and we still fell. You can't blame us for not trying." They fail to see that, just like Gerstner at IBM, leaders atop companies in the late stages of decline need to get back to a calm, clear-headed, and focused approach. If you want to reverse decline, be rigorous about what *not* to do. In the early 1990s, I invited a former Marine turned entrepreneur to guest-lecture in my course on creativity at the Stanford Graduate School of Business. He'd done multiple tours of jungle combat in the Vietnam War. When asked what lessons, if any, carried over to his civilian life as an entrepreneur, he thought about it for a moment and then responded, "When you have just a few people, and there is enemy all around you, the best thing is to say, 'You take this section from here to here, and you take this section from here to here, and *do not* fire on automatic. Take one shot at a time.'"

Breathe. Calm yourself. Think. Focus. Aim. Take *one shot at a time*. Otherwise, you can find yourself in some version of the calamity that befell Addressograph Corporation, the once-leader in office addressing and duplicating machines. Every $10,000 invested in Addressograph at the start of 1945 and held through 1960 generated half a million dollars.[129] In 1965, however, Xerox introduced the 2400 copier, a direct threat to Addressograph's duplicating products. Panicking, Addressograph launched a crash program, releasing twenty-three new products in three years. It lost track of billing and accounts receivable, creating $70 million in late, unpaid, and untraceable customer orders strewn about, scrawled on scraps of paper and backs of envelopes. Sixteen of the twenty-three new products failed.[130]

When profitability declined through the early 1970s and culminated in losses, the board grasped for a visionary CEO from
the outside. An aggressive "go-getter," the new leader threw the
company into a traumatic reinvention, a complete psychological
transformation, a corporate revolution. In his view, Addressograph "was like a boat going in circles in a lake that was going
dry," a situation requiring "massive change in as short a period
as possible." [131] He boldly "shed the barnacles of the past" and
launched a salvation strategy, leaping into the Office of the
Future with word processing and electronic office machines.[132]
But the leap did not go as planned, and Addressograph's visionary savior faced an unhappy board. For three hours, he defended
his leadership, citing statistics and pointing to achievements. At
the end of his impassioned presentation, a board member mo-
tioned that he step down.[133] Ten months later, in 1981, Addressograph posted single-year losses that wiped out nearly *all* of a
half a century's worth of accumulated net worth.[134]

You might be wondering, But wait a minute! Surely, Addressograph is the buggy-whip story all over again. The company's
mechanical duplicating machines became obsolete in the face of
Xerox's technology, and the world just passed them by.

And on one hand, you would be correct: its clinkity-clankity
product lines *had* become obsolete, obliterated by a technology
disruption. But the fundamental need for its core capability, the
offset-duplicating business, had not become obsolete. Even as I
write these words in 2008, nearly half a century after Xerox
launched its copier line, offset printing remains the primary solution for high-volume, high-quality print jobs. Addressograph
would have had to migrate out of the office environment (where
Xerox would win in small-run, one-off duplicating), but it had

already made successful inroads in commercial printing by the early 1970s. Unfortunately, Addressograph lurched about in fearful, frantic reaction while neglecting the offset business and never regained momentum in its core business.[135] Like the climber who lets go of his brake hand, Addressograph's panicky behavior sent the company hurtling over the cliff.

In a frenzy of inconsistency—flip-flopping from one new strategy to another, moving across the country to a new headquarters and then back across the country to yet a third headquarters (from Cleveland to Los Angeles, from Los Angeles to Chicago)—Addressograph churned through four CEOs and endured two bankruptcies in fewer than a dozen years.[136] One CEO left in such a hurry that an employee described his departure as like having a brain surgeon leave in the middle of an operation.[137]

By the late 1990s, the ranks had dwindled from 30,000 employees to just a few hundred, while every dollar invested at the start of 1980 was now worth less than five cents. Summed up one longtime analyst of the company, "It's been almost like a guy who contracts a fatal disease. I've just watched it shrivel up and die. It's very sad."[138] Addressograph had plummeted through Stage 4 to enter the final stage, Capitulation to Irrelevance or Death.

MARKERS FOR STAGE 4

- **A SERIES OF SILVER BULLETS:** There is a tendency to make dramatic, big moves, such as a "game changing" acquisition or a discontinuous leap into a new strategy or an exciting innovation, in an attempt to quickly catalyze a breakthrough—and then to do it again and again, lurching about from program to program, goal to goal, strategy to strategy, in a pattern of chronic inconsistency.

- **GRASPING FOR A LEADER-AS-SAVIOR:** The board responds to threats and setbacks by searching for a charismatic leader and/ or outside savior.

- **PANIC AND HASTE:** Instead of being calm, deliberate, and disciplined, people exhibit hasty, reactive behavior, bordering on panic.

- **RADICAL CHANGE AND "REVOLUTION" WITH FANFARE:** The language of "revolution" and "radical" change characterizes the new era: New programs! New cultures! New strategies! Leaders engage in hoopla, spending a lot of energy trying to align and "motivate" people, engaging in buzzwords and taglines.

- **HYPE PRECEDES RESULTS:** Instead of setting expectations low—underscoring the duration and difficulty of the turnaround—leaders hype their visions; they "sell the future" to compensate for the lack of current results, initiating a pattern of overpromising and underdelivering.

- **INITIAL UPSWING FOLLOWED BY DISAPPOINTMENTS:** There is an initial burst of positive results, but they do not last; dashed hope follows dashed hope; the organization achieves no buildup, no cumulative momentum.

- **CONFUSION AND CYNICISM:** People cannot easily articulate what the organization stands for; core values have eroded to the point of irrelevance; the organization has become "just another place to work," a place to get a paycheck; people lose faith in their ability to triumph and prevail. Instead of passionately believing in the organization's core values and purpose, people become distrustful, regarding visions and values as little more than PR and rhetoric.

- **CHRONIC RESTRUCTURING AND EROSION OF FINANCIAL STRENGTH:** Each failed initiative drains resources; cash flow and financial liquidity begin to decline; the organization undergoes multiple restructurings; options narrow and strategic decisions are increasingly dictated by circumstance.

STAGE 5:
CAPITULATION TO
IRRELEVANCE OR DEATH

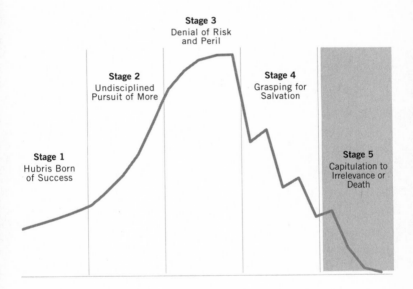

Stage 3
Denial of Risk
and Peril

Stage 2
Undisciplined
Pursuit of More

Stage 4
Grasping for
Salvation

Stage 1
Hubris Born
of Success

Stage 5
Capitulation to
Irrelevance or
Death

In researching the final stages of decline, looking at the capitulation of once-towering companies, I kept thinking about how Professor Bill Lazier began his course on small business management at the Stanford Graduate School of Business. He'd walk into class and begin cold-calling students.

"What's the central issue in the case?" he'd push.

Students who had worked at large companies, consulting firms, and investment banks gave answers like "their strategic choices" or "identifying their value chain" or "developing a brand" or any number of other smart-sounding MBA answers.

Unsatisfied by vacuous buzzwords, Lazier would keep pressing, pacing back and forth across the classroom. "No! Think!"

Finally, some student would venture forth, "Well, I don't know if this is what you're looking for, but they can't make payroll next week. The company is going to run out of cash."

Lazier would stop his pacing, walk over to the blank chalkboard, and write in giant letters (and I mean giant, at least two-feet high) one word: **CASH**.

"Never forget," Lazier would say. "You pay your bills with cash. You can be profitable and bankrupt."

You can be profitable and bankrupt. The idea had never occurred to most students who'd worked in big companies. In the entrepreneurial phase, leaders struggle just to get enough cash to become self-sustaining, but as an organization becomes big and successful, cash consciousness atrophies. Leaders in successful companies worry more about earnings. But organizations do not die from lack of earnings. They die from lack of cash.

While editing this piece in late 2008, I'm looking at a stunning news story: General Motors, the monumental symbol of American Corporate Power, is seeking salvation from the government, standing on the verge of late Stage 4 as it runs short on cash. Even for a company that had once been the largest corporation in the world, Lazier's lesson can hit full force: you pay your bills with cash.

As institutions hurtle toward Stage 5, they spiral downward, increasingly out of control. Each cycle—grasping followed by disappointment followed by more grasping—erodes resources. Cash tightens. Hope fades. Options narrow.

We found two basic versions of Stage 5. In the first version, those in power come to believe that capitulation offers a better overall outcome than continuing to fight. In the second version, those in power continue the struggle, but they run out of options, and the enterprise either dies outright or shrinks into utter irrelevance compared to its previous grandeur. Let's look at two companies, one that chose to give up the fight and sell out, and the other that fought on, only to go bankrupt.

GIVING UP THE FIGHT

By the late 1980s, Scott Paper had fallen so far behind P&G and Kimberly-Clark that it had little choice but to take on huge debt to reinvest in a series of last-gasp efforts to catch up. Its debt-to-equity ratio jumped to average 175 percent from 1985 to 1994. Capital constraints led to chronic restructuring and cost cutting: $167 million in 1990, $249 million in 1991, and another $490 million in early 1994. Scott's debt rating fell to just one step above junk bonds.[139] And that's when the board brought in Rambo Al.

When analyst Kathryn McAuley heard the news that Al

Dunlap had been named CEO of Scott Paper in 1994, she did some quick research on his track record. "I said to myself: 'Well, the board sold the company.' " [140] Dunlap became infamous for his nickname, "Rambo in Pinstripes," an image reinforced when he posed for a photograph sporting black paint under his eyes, bandoliers, and two very real-looking mock automatic weapons, while also garbed in a white dress shirt and a lion-emblazoned necktie.[141] Dunlap slashed more than 11,000 jobs, including 71 percent of upper management. Profits rebounded as cost cutting flowed directly to the bottom line, and Dunlap capitalized on the moment to sell the once-proud Scott Paper to archrival Kimberly-Clark.

It would be easy to focus on how corporate Rambo Al Dunlap made eight figures for less than two years' effort and how he justified his pay by writing, "I'm a superstar in my field, much like Michael Jordan in basketball and Bruce Springsteen in rock 'n' roll. My pay should be compared to superstars in other fields, not to the average CEO." [142] But Dunlap, for all his pugnacious bravado, was simply the mechanism of Scott Paper's capitulation, not its cause. Had Scott Paper not fallen through Stages 1, 2, 3, and 4—and had Scott Paper not lost control of its financial freedom—Dunlap would have never been brought in to burn the village in order to save it.

No company we studied was destined to fall all the way to Stage 5, and each company could have made different decisions earlier in the journey to reverse its downward slide. But by the time a company has moved through Stages 1, 2, 3, and 4, those in power can become exhausted and dispirited, and eventually abandon hope. And when you abandon hope, you should begin preparing for the end.

But hope alone is not enough; you need enough resources to continue the fight. If you lose the ability to make strategic choices, forced into short-term survival decisions that cripple the enterprise, then the odds of full recovery become increasingly remote. That's exactly what we see in the long, tragic demise of one of America's great success stories, Zenith Corporation.

RUNNING OUT OF OPTIONS

Zenith's rise to greatness dates back to the first half of the twentieth century, when eccentric mastermind Eugene McDonald led Zenith to dominant positions in radio and television. In June 1945, *Fortune* ran a big spread titled "Commander McDonald of Zenith" and featured a full-page photo of McDonald posing with artifacts from his world-traveling adventures: a marine clock, guns, Eskimo relics, and even a stuffed penguin that used to be his pet. The article showcased McDonald fishing in the

Caribbean, navigating his yacht in a dashing sea cap given to him by a European count, paddling a kayak with Eskimos, hunting pirate treasure in the Pacific, examining ancient bones from a dig, preparing to pilot a glider, working his Mexican gold mine, and reading *National Geographic* aloud to his children.[143] Visionary and frenetic, McDonald applied his genius to business, pioneering portable home radios and moving Zenith into television during the industry's early days.

Zenith entered Stage 1, Hubris Born of Success, late in the McDonald era. Zenith became the #1 manufacturer of black-and-white televisions, and every dollar invested in Zenith at the start of 1950 and held through 1965 increased in value more than one hundred times, generating cumulative returns more than ten times the market. When Japanese televisions began to gain market traction, Zenith arrogantly ignored the Japanese threat. In Zenith's view, the Japanese (the *Japanese*, for goodness' sake, with their cheap products) could not possibly pose a serious threat to the Great American Quality Brand, captured in the tagline "Zenith—The Quality Goes In Before The Name Goes On."[144]

Zenith moved through Stage 2, Undisciplined Pursuit of More, in the late 1960s and early 1970s. After achieving its goal to surpass RCA as the #1 maker of color television sets, Zenith invested in a massive increase in manufacturing capacity that doubled its debt-to-equity ratio to 100 percent. Zenith also experienced a problematic succession of power. Commander McDonald left the company in the hands of a septuagenarian CEO, with Zenith's counsel Joseph Wright as president. Wright eventually moved into the CEO role, but when his chosen successor died, Wright faced limited succession options. Zenith brought in an outsider from Ford, who eventually became chairman.[145]

Zenith moved into Stage 3, Denial of Risk and Peril, externalizing blame (pointing out the window to Japanese trade practices, the struggling U.S. economy, labor unrest, oil shocks, and so forth) rather than confronting its own lack of competitiveness. Saddled with excess capacity, Zenith lowered prices in a battle for market share and took on more debt, both of which drove its profitability ratios down to levels not seen in thirty years.[146]

Zenith fell into Stage 4, Grasping for Salvation, in the late 1970s, when it leapt at a slew of opportunities all at the same time. "If we have any plan at all, it's that we'll take a shot at everything," explained a Zenith senior leader to *Business Week*. Zenith jumped into VCRs, videodiscs, telephones that linked through televisions, home-security video cameras, cable TV decoders, and personal computers. To fund all these moves, Zenith drove its debt-to-equity ratio to 140 percent.[147]

But this unhappy saga does not end there. Amazingly, given its scattershot grasping for salvation, Zenith stumbled by luck upon a new opportunity that nearly made the company great again, the newly formed Data Systems unit headed by the energetic Jerry Pearlman. Brilliant and articulate, a cum laude graduate from Princeton who'd finished in the top 2 percent of his class at Harvard Business School, Pearlman had been called a "corporate visionary" by *Business Week*.[148] Pearlman became CEO and led Zenith to become the #2 maker of IBM-compatible personal computers, and in a stroke of prescient genius, staked out a leading position for Zenith in the emerging laptop market.

From 1980 to 1989, the Data Systems Division increased its revenues thirtyfold, generating more than 50 percent of Zenith's total revenues and nearly all of Zenith's profits. Zenith could have become Dell or Compaq.[149]

But Zenith still had the television business, and after all those years of denial and grasping for salvation, Zenith's financial condition had deteriorated; cash on hand had dropped to less than 5 percent of current liabilities. Pearlman tried to sell the television business but didn't get the price he wanted. A few years earlier, before it ran out of cash, Zenith might have had the opportunity to close down the television business, channel all its remaining resources into the Data Systems Division, and turn itself into one of the great computer companies. Instead, exhausted, harried by angry shareholders, and burdened by Zenith's half a billion dollars of debt and shrinking cash reserves, Pearlman found himself running out of options. On September 29, 1989, Pearlman met Bull Corporation CEO Francis Lorentz at a Paris restaurant to consummate the sale of Zenith's computer business to Bull. Lorentz later commented that Pearlman simply looked "relieved." To his credit, Pearlman tried to rebuild Zenith after selling the computer flywheel, but the television business just kept dragging Zenith down, generating year upon year of losses, and in 1995, Pearlman stepped down.[150]

You might think that companies fall all the way to the bottom because their leaders make just-plain-stupid decisions. But through Zenith's story, we see how even some of the smartest and most capable leaders can find themselves unable to control their company's destiny if the accumulated impact of Stages 1 through 4 destroys their cash position. After Pearlman, Zenith churned through five CEOs in ten years, fell into bankruptcy, and reemerged with less than 400 employees, 98 percent fewer than the 36,000 employed in 1988. It had fallen from one of the greatest success stories of American business history at mid-century into just a shadow of its former self.[151]

DENIAL OR HOPE

Not all companies deserve to last. Perhaps society is better off getting rid of organizations that have fallen from great to terrible rather than continuing to let them inflict their massive inadequacies on their stakeholders. Institutional self-perpetuation holds no legitimate place in a world of scarce resources; institutional mediocrity should be terminated, or transformed into excellence.

When should a company continue to fight, and when does refusal to capitulate become just another form of denial? Perhaps the Scott Paper board made a wise decision to surrender the company's independence rather than watch it die a slow, painful death or atrophy into irrelevance. And perhaps Zenith would have been better off had it capitulated earlier to a willing buyer, before mounting debt forced its hand. If you cannot marshal a compelling answer to the question, "What would be lost, and how would the world be worse off, if we ceased to exist?" then perhaps capitulation is the wise path. But if you have a clear and inspired purpose built upon solid core values, then the noble course may be to fight on, to reverse decline, and to try to rekindle greatness.

The point of the struggle is not just to survive, but to build an enterprise that makes such a distinctive impact on the world it touches, and does so with such superior performance, that it would leave a gaping hole—a hole that could not be easily filled by any other institution—if it ceased to exist. To accomplish this requires leaders who retain faith that they can find a way to prevail in pursuit of a cause larger than mere survival (and larger than themselves), while also maintaining the stoic will needed to take whatever actions must be taken, however excruciating, for the sake of that cause. This is the very type of leader who finds a path out of the darkness and gives us well-founded hope. And it is to that type of leadership that we now turn.

WELL-FOUNDED HOPE

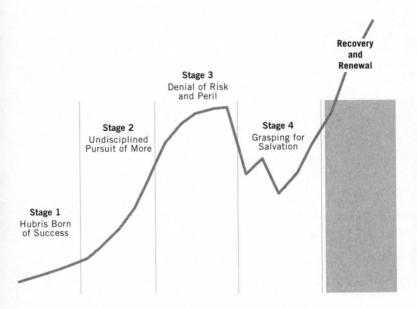

Recovery and Renewal

Stage 3
Denial of Risk and Peril

Stage 2
Undisciplined Pursuit of More

Stage 4
Grasping for Salvation

Stage 1
Hubris Born of Success

When Anne Mulcahy became chief executive of Xerox in 2001, she inherited a company mired in Stage 4. Digesting a $273 million loss, Xerox stock had dropped 92 percent in less than two years, wiping out more than $38 billion in shareholder value. With Xerox's debt-to-equity ratio exceeding 900 percent, Moody's rated its bonds as junk. The Securities and Exchange

Commission had launched an investigation into Xerox's books, which precluded Xerox from registering any securities and limited its fundraising options. With $19 billion in debt and only $100 million in cash, Mulcahy described the situation as "terrifying." Prior to Mulcahy's appointment, Xerox had strived to reinvent itself for the Digital Age, hiring superstar Richard Thoman from IBM (where he'd been a valued member of Gerstner's team) to succeed CEO Paul Allaire, who remained chairman. "We were looking for a change agent," Allaire said of the decision to go outside. But Thoman lasted only thirteen months as CEO.[152]

In May 2000, Mulcahy had finished packing for a business trip to Tokyo when Allaire asked her to come to his office right away. "Here's the deal," said Allaire. "Rick's [Thoman] out. I'm coming back in as CEO, and I want you to be president and COO of Xerox, and a year later, if things are right, you'll be CEO."[153]

Mulcahy had never planned or expected to become CEO, describing her ascension as a total surprise.[154] "The board probably sat back and said, 'What choice do we have?' So I can't say it was a roaring endorsement," Mulcahy later told writer Kevin Maney. "It probably was a little bit of a last resort."[155] The consummate insider, she'd worked nearly a quarter of a century at Xerox in sales and human resources, never drawing outside attention; Mulcahy didn't even appear in *Fortune* magazine's "50 Most Powerful Women in Business" ranking the year before becoming president.[156]

Mulcahy could have perpetuated a Stage 4 doom loop by setting forth to utterly smash the culture and revolutionize the company overnight. But instead, she retorted to those who said she would need to kill the culture to save the company, "I *am* the culture. If I can't figure out how to bring the culture with me, I'm the wrong person for the job."[157] For Mulcahy, it was all about Xerox, not about her. When *Newsweek* called her, Mulcahy declined to be interviewed about her management style.[158] In fact, we found only four feature articles about Mulcahy during her first three years as CEO, a surprisingly small number, given how few women become CEO of storied Fortune 500 companies.[159]

Some observers questioned whether this insider, this unknown team player who had Xerox DNA baked into her chromosomes, would have the ferocious will needed to save the company.[160] They needn't have worried. Their first clue might have come in reading her favorite book, Caroline Alexander's *The Endurance,* which chronicles how, against all odds, adventurer Ernest Shackleton rescued his men after their ship splintered into thousands of pieces as Antarctic ice crushed in around it in 1916. Accompanied by five crew members, Shackleton navigated 800 miles of violent seas in a 22-foot lifeboat to find help for the remaining survivors.[161] Drawing inspiration from Shackleton, Mulcahy didn't take a weekend off for two years.[162] She shut down a number of businesses, including the inkjet-printer unit that she'd championed earlier in her career, and cut $2.5 billion out of Xerox's cost structure. Not that she found these decisions easy—"I don't think I want them to get easy," she later reflected—but they were necessary to stave off utter catastrophe.[163] During its darkest days, Xerox faced the very real threat of bankruptcy, yet Mulcahy rebuffed with steely silence her advisors' repeated suggestions that she consider Chapter 11. She also held fast against a torrent of advice from outsiders to cut R&D to save the company, noting that a return to greatness depended on both tough cost cutting and long-term investment, and actually *increased* R&D as a percentage of sales during the darkest days. "For me, this was all about having a company that people could retire from, having a company that their kids could come and work at, having a company that actually would have pride some day in terms of its accomplishments." [164]

For 2000 and 2001, Xerox posted a total of nearly $367 million in losses. By 2006, Xerox posted profits in excess of $1 billion and sported a much stronger balance sheet. And in 2008, *Chief Executive* magazine selected Mulcahy as chief executive of the year. At the time of this writing in 2008, Xerox's transition had been going strong for seven years—no guarantee, of course, that Xerox will continue to climb, but an impressive recovery from the early 2000s.[165]

Xerox. Nucor. IBM. Texas Instruments. Pitney Bowes. Nordstrom. Disney. Boeing. HP. Merck. What do these companies have in common? Every one took at least one tremendous fall at some point in its history and recovered. Sometimes the tumble came early, when they were small and vulnerable, and sometimes the tumble came when they were large, established enterprises. But in every case, leaders emerged who broke the trajectory of decline and simply refused to give up on the idea of not only survival, but of ultimate triumph despite the most extreme odds. And like Mulcahy, these leaders used decline as a catalyst. As Dick Clark, the quiet, longtime head of Merck manufacturing who became CEO after Gilmartin, put it, "A crisis is a terrible thing to waste." [166]

If we discovered that organizational decline is a function first and foremost of forces out of our control—and if we discovered that those who fall will inevitably keep falling to their doom—we could rightly indulge in despair. But that is not our conclusion from this analysis, not if you catch decline in Stages 1, 2, or 3. And in some cases, you might even be able to reverse course once in Stage 4, as long as you still have enough resources to get out of the cycle of grasping and rebuild one step at a time.

If you have not yet fallen, beware the temptation to proclaim a crisis when none exists. Recall the Gerstner philosophy: the right leaders feel a sense of urgency in good times and bad, whether facing threat or opportunity, no matter what. They're obsessed, afflicted with a creative compulsion and inner drive for progress—burning hot coals in the stomach—that remain constant whether facing threat or not. To manufacture a crisis when none exists, to shriek that we're all standing on a "burning platform" soon to collapse in a spectacular conflagration, creates cynicism. The right people will drive improvement, whether standing on a burning platform or not, and they never take well to manipulation.

And if you've already taken a fall and you do face a genuine crisis, the sooner you break the cycle of grasping for salvation the better. The path to recovery lies first and foremost in returning to sound management practices and rigorous strategic thinking. In Appendix 6, I've outlined three cases of great companies that fell and recovered (IBM, Nucor, and Nordstrom), and I've laid out their recovery through the lens of the good-to-great framework of disciplines (summarized in Appendix 7). If you seek a refresher course on management discipline, it never hurts to review the classics, including Drucker, Porter, Deming, and Peters/Waterman. Of course, you have to stop the bleeding first and make sure you don't run out of cash, but that's simply emergency surgery, not full recovery. The point being, however you slice it, lack of management discipline correlates with decline, and passionate adherence to management discipline correlates with recovery and ascent.

All that said, there remains a question: what about "the perennial gale of creative destruction" as described by the famous twentieth-century economist Joseph Schumpeter, wherein technological change and visionary entrepreneurs upend and destroy the old order and create a new order, only to see their new order destroyed and replaced by an even newer order, in an endless cycle of chaos and upheaval?[167] Perhaps all social institutions in our modern world face disruptive forces so fast, big, and unpredictable that every entity will fall within years or decades, without exception. Can we still stave off decline in the face of severe turbulence?

While working on *How the Mighty Fall*, my colleague Morten Hansen and I have been simultaneously working on a six-year research project to study companies that grew from vulnerability to greatness in severe environments characterized by rapid and unpredictable change in contrast to others that did not prevail *in the same brutally turbulent environments*. Consider the following analogy: Suppose you wake up in base camp at the foot of Mount Everest and a big storm rolls through. You can hunker down in the safety of your tent and let the storm pass by. But if you wake up as a vulnerable little speck at 27,000 feet on the side of the mountain, where the storms are bigger and faster moving, the environment severe and unforgiving, and everything more uncertain and uncontrollable, then a storm just might kill you. We believe most leaders in every sector feel they are metaphorically moving higher on the mountain, into increasingly turbulent and unforgiving environments.

This new research is enlarging our understanding of the principles and strategies needed to prevail in a turbulent world, and I'd like to preview a key conclusion here, one that pertains directly to the question of corporate decline. When the world spins out of control, when external tumult threatens to upend our best-laid plans, does our destiny remain in our own hands? Or must we accept that creative destruction reigns supreme and that success will be short and fleeting, even for the very best? Our research shows that it is possible to build a great institution that sustains exceptional performance for multiple decades, perhaps longer, even in the face of chaos, disruption, uncertainty, and violent change. In fact, our research shows that if you've been practicing the principles of greatness all the way along, *you should get down on your knees and pray for severe turbulence*, for that's when you can pull even further ahead of those who lack your relentless intensity. But beware: if you get caught in the stages of decline during turbulent times—if you succumb to hubris, overreaching, denial, and grasping for quick fixes—your fall will be faster and more violent than in stable times. The nearly overnight demise of some of America's largest financial companies in 2008 illustrates just how fast the mighty can fall in a highly turbulent world.

If you've fallen into decline, get back to solid management disciplines—now! And if you're still strong, be vigilant for early markers of decline. But above all, do not ever capitulate to the idea that an era of success must inevitably be followed by decline and demise brought on by forces outside your control. The matched-pair contrast method that we employ in our research (comparing successful outcomes to unsuccessful outcomes, controlling as much as possible to pick similar companies facing similar environmental conditions) yields an important insight: circumstances alone do not determine outcomes. Of course, there always remains the chance of a random catastrophe, and life offers no 100-percent guarantees; after all, you can be the healthiest, most relentless athlete of all time and still be stricken with a crippling disease or career-ending accident. But setting that aside, the main message of our work remains: we are not imprisoned by our circumstances, our setbacks, our history, our mistakes, or even staggering defeats along the way. We are freed by our choices.

> The signature of the truly great versus the merely successful is not the absence of difficulty, but the ability to come back from setbacks, even cataclysmic catastrophes, stronger than before. Great nations can decline and recover. Great companies can fall and recover. Great social institutions can fall and recover. And great individuals can fall and recover. As long as you never get entirely knocked out of the game, there remains always hope.

We all need beacons of light as we struggle with the inevitable setbacks of life and work. For me, that light has often come from studying Winston Churchill. In the early 1930s, Churchill's career had descended into what biographer Virginia Cowles called "a quagmire from which there seemed to be no rescue." Entering his late fifties, fattening up, and losing hair, he'd been widely blamed for Britain's financial dislocation in the Depression, having put Britain back on the gold standard as the chancellor of the Exchequer. He'd broken with his party, isolating himself from the mainstream by his opposition to Indian self-rule, refusing even to meet with Gandhi. He'd been forever tagged as the architect of the World War I tragedy at Gallipoli (a botched plan to knock Turkey out of the war, and to attack Germany and Austria from the southeast), which cost 213,980 British casualties for zero gain; even though the Dardanelles Commission cleared him of blame, he remained tainted by the disaster. The 1929 stock market crash cost Churchill a considerable fortune. And on December 12, 1931, he stepped off a curb on Fifth Avenue in New York, looking to his right to check for traffic as he would in London rather than to his left as he needed to in America. Passers-by heard a sickening "thwaump!" as a car driving more than 30 miles per hour blindsided Churchill, knocking him yards down Fifth Avenue. The accident threw him into the hospital, a long recovery, and a severe depression.[168]

At the end of Volume I of his series, *The Last Lion*, William Manchester captures Churchill's position in 1932. Lady Astor visited with Joseph Stalin, who quizzed her on the political landscape in Britain. Astor prattled on about the powerful, the up-and-coming, naming Neville Chamberlain as the star.

"What about Churchill?" asked Stalin.

"Churchill?" Astor's eyes widened. Then with a disdainful wrinkle of her nose, "Oh, he's finished." [169]

Eight years later, on June 4, 1940, Churchill stood in front of

Parliament as prime minister while Hitler's Panzer divisions swept across France. Poland: gone. Belgium: gone. Holland: gone. Norway: gone. Denmark: gone. France: collapsing. England: reeling from the rout leading up to the evacuation from Dunkirk. Most world leaders, including many in Britain, saw no choice but to cede Europe to the Nazis. Churchill's rivals expected Churchill to see no other alternative than a negotiated peace with Herr Hitler and his Nazi henchmen, and they hoped to capitalize on his taking the political fallout for capitulation.

They were to be disappointed.

Clutching his notes, for he always feared that without his carefully prepared text he would be at a loss for words, Churchill glowered out across the House of Commons and issued his famous words, "We shall never surrender, and even if, which I do not for a moment believe, this Island or a large part of it were subjugated and starving, then our Empire beyond the seas, armed and guarded by the British Fleet, would carry on the struggle, until, in God's good time, the New World, with all its power and might, steps forth to the rescue and the liberation of the old." [170]

Not only would Churchill redeem himself by giving voice to Britain's resolve to stand against the Axis powers, he would also go on to win the Nobel Prize in literature, return again as prime minister at age seventy-seven, be knighted by the Queen, and sear into Cold War lexicon the term "Iron Curtain" in his prescient warning about Soviet aggression.

In 1941, during England's sternest days, Churchill returned to his old school Harrow, where he'd received embarrassingly low scores, to give a commencement address. The headmaster cast worried glances at Churchill, who had fallen asleep, slumbering through most of the ceremony. But when introduced, Churchill made his way to the podium, stared out over the assemblage of boys, and gave his commencement message, "This is the lesson: never give in, never give in, never, never, never, never—in nothing, great or small, large or petty—never give in except to convictions of honour and good sense. Never yield to force; never yield to the apparently overwhelming might of the enemy."[171]

Never give in. Be willing to change tactics, but never give up your core purpose. Be willing to kill failed business ideas, even to shutter big operations you've been in for a long time, but never give up on the idea of building a great company. Be willing to evolve into an entirely different portfolio of activities, even to the point of zero overlap with what you do today, but never give up on the principles that define your culture. Be willing to embrace the inevitability of creative destruction, but never give up on the discipline to create your own future. Be willing to embrace loss, to endure pain, to temporarily lose freedoms, but never give up faith in the ability to prevail. Be willing to form alliances with former adversaries, to accept necessary compromise, but never—ever—give up on your core values.

The path out of darkness begins with those exasperatingly persistent individuals who are constitutionally incapable of capitulation. It's one thing to suffer a staggering defeat—as will likely happen to every enduring business and social enterprise at some point in its history—and entirely another to give up on the values and aspirations that make the protracted struggle worthwhile. Failure is not so much a physical state as a state of mind; success is falling down, and getting up one more time, without end.

Appendices

APPENDIX 1:

FALLEN-COMPANY SELECTION CRITERIA

Our research process involves selecting cases to study based on objective, preset criteria. We do not decide which companies we "want" to study and then look to find a time frame during which their data meets a pattern. Rather, we lay out the criteria for the study-set selection before we see the data and systematically eliminate companies from consideration based on whether they meet the criteria. The following is a summary of the steps we went through to arrive at the final study set of fallen companies. (Cumulative stock-return calculations determined using data from the following source: ©200601 CRSP®, Center for Research in Security Prices. Graduate School of Business, The University of Chicago. Used with permission. All rights reserved. www.crsp.chicagobooth.edu.)

STARTING UNIVERSE

Sixty corporations representing more than thirty industry sectors, drawn from the research database used for the *Good to Great* and *Built to Last* research efforts.

3M	A&P	Abbott Labs	Addressograph
American Express	Ames	Bank of America	Bethlehem Steel
Boeing	Bristol-Myers Squibb	Burroughs	Chase Manhattan
Chrysler	Circuit City	Citicorp	Colgate
Columbia Pictures	Eckerd	Fannie Mae	Ford
GE	Gillette	GM	Great Western
Harris	Hasbro	Hewlett-Packard (HP)	Howard Johnson
IBM	Johnson & Johnson	Kenwood	Kimberly-Clark
Kroger	Marriott	McDonnell Douglas	Melville
Merck	Motorola	Nordstrom	Norton
Nucor	Pfizer	Philip Morris	Pitney Bowes
Procter & Gamble	R.J. Reynolds	Rubbermaid	Scott Paper
Silo	Sony	Teledyne	Texas Instruments
Upjohn	Walgreens	Wal-Mart	Walt Disney
Warner-Lambert	Wells Fargo	Westinghouse	Zenith

CRITERION 1: CANDIDATES FOR BEING
A GREAT COMPANY AT SOME POINT IN HISTORY

A company qualifies as a candidate if it meets *any one* of the following conditions, a, b, or c:

a) Selected as a visionary company in *Built to Last* or a good-to-great company in *Good to Great*.

b) Selected as a comparison company in *Built to Last* or *Good to Great*, and had a fifteen-year period of cumulative stock returns that exceeded the general market by 3X at some point in the company's history. Note that our research method involves studying companies during specific eras in history when they met particular performance criteria. Companies can achieve high performance during one era and fall during a later era (the subject of this study); similarly, companies can deliver sub-par performance during one era and then make a leap to exceptional performance during a later era (the subject of the good-to-great study).

    i. Exception: if the candidate met Criterion 1b only in the final twelve months before being acquired, it should be excluded because its stock returns may have been artificially driven upward due to takeover speculation.

    ii. Exception: if the candidate attained its above-3X performance over fifteen years only as a "spike pattern" rather than a sustained run of performance, it should be excluded. The test for a "spike pattern" over any given fifteen-year period is as follows: (1) Calculate the percentage increase in cumulative returns relative to the general market over the fifteen-year cycle during which the company beat the market by more than 3X; (2) Calculate the percentage increase in cumulative returns from the start of the fifteen-year performance run to exactly ten years into the run; and (3) If the ratio of calculation 2 divided by calculation 1 is 0.20 or lower, then the cycle counts as a "spike pattern." The table below illustrates the spike pattern calculations.

	Example Case 1	Example Case 2
Start of 15-year, above-3X run	1.0X the market	1.0X the market
10 years into 15-year run	1.25X the market	1.75X the market
15 years into 15-year run	4.0X the market	3.1X the market
Calculation 2	25 percent	75 percent
Calculation 1	300 percent	210 percent
Ratio of 2 divided by 1	0.08	0.36
Conclusion	Spike Pattern	*Not* a Spike Pattern

iii. Exception: if the candidate showed more negative years than positive years during the 3X-plus, fifteen-year performance phase, then eliminate it.

c) For comparison companies where we do not have stock return data going back far enough to assess returns during the company's strongest years, we can marshal overwhelming evidence that the company had attained significant success prior to the availability of CRSP data. The evidence needs to fall into three categories: (1) evidence of financial results that establish the company as one of the largest and most successful companies in its industry, (2) evidence that the company had a significant impact on the development of its industry during its greatest years, and (3) evidence that the company had maintained a strong performance and made a significant impact for at least two decades.

Companies eliminated: Chase Manhattan, Columbia Pictures, Great Western, Howard Johnson, Kenwood, Norton, Silo, R.J. Reynolds, and Upjohn.

CRITERION 2: CANDIDATES FOR DECLINE— FROM GREAT COMPANY TO MEDIOCRITY OR WORSE

Take the companies that made it through Cut 1. From these, a company qualifies as a candidate if it meets either of the following conditions:

a) Selected as a visionary company in *Built to Last* or a good-to-great company in *Good to Great*, and had a negative inflection from 1995 to 2005. A "negative inflection" in this case is defined as generating cumulative stock returns at or below 0.80X the general market from January 1, 1995, to January 1, 2005.

b) Selected as a comparison company in *Built to Last* or *Good to Great*, and showed cumulative stock returns at or below 0.80X the general market over a ten-year period (or up to the point of being acquired or going bankrupt, if the decline lasted less than ten years) and the company failed to regain cumulative stock returns of 3X the general market over a fifteen-year period later in its history.

Companies eliminated: 3M, Abbott Labs, American Express, Boeing, Chrysler, Citicorp, Colgate, Fannie Mae, Ford, GE, Gillette, Harris, IBM, Johnson & Johnson, Kimberly-Clark, Kroger, Marriott, Nordstrom, Pfizer, Philip Morris, Pitney Bowes, Procter & Gamble, Texas Instruments, Walgreens, Wal-Mart, Warner-Lambert, and Wells Fargo.

CRITERION 3: OTHER EXCLUSIONS

Exclusion for Industry Effect: if there is significant question as to whether the performance pattern was due primarily to an industry effect, then eliminate the company.

Exclusion for Founder Effect: if the only period of ascent occurred during the reign of a single founder, and the company began a sustained fall within one year after that individual founder departed, then eliminate the company.

Exclusion for Pre-1950: if the company's period of great performance ended prior to 1950, and there isn't enough data to carefully examine its rise-and-fall period, then eliminate the company.

Exclusion for Chronic Decline: if the company demonstrated a multi-decade chronic pattern of decline prior to its upswing that would call into question whether it was a great company before its fall, then eliminate the company.

Companies eliminated: Bethlehem Steel, Bristol-Myers Squibb, Burroughs, Eckerd, GM, Hasbro, McDonnell Douglas, Melville, Nucor, Sony, Teledyne, Walt Disney, and Westinghouse.

FINAL STUDY SET, FALLEN CASES

Company	Era of Focus for Analysis of Decline	Total Time Frame
A&P	1950s–1970s	1859–1998
Addressograph	1960s–1980s	1896–1998
Ames	1980s–1990s	1958–2002
Bank of America	1970s–1980s	1904–1998
Circuit City	1990s–2000s	1949–2008
HP	1990s–2000s	1937–2008
Merck	1990s–2000s	1891–2008
Motorola	1990s–2000s	1927–2008
Rubbermaid	1980s–1990s	1920–1998
Scott Paper	1960s–1990s	1879–1995
Zenith	1960s–1980s	1923–2000

APPENDIX 2:

SUCCESS-CONTRAST SELECTION CRITERIA

The cornerstone of our research methodology lies in studying contrasts between highly successful and less successful outcomes. In this analysis, we adapted the contrast methodology to pick success-contrast companies to compare with the companies that fell. Each success contrast attained and/or sustained exceptional results during the era that the corresponding fallen company had its negative inflection. Six cases already had success contrasts selected from previous research studies (A&P, Addressograph, Ames, Bank of America, Scott Paper, and Zenith). For the remaining cases, we implemented the following selection and scoring process. We identified a set of potential success-contrast candidates based on other companies that were in the same or similar businesses at the contrast-selection year.* To identify

---

* The contrast-selection year for Circuit City, HP, Merck, and Motorola is 1995; for Rubbermaid it is 1992.

success-contrast candidates, we used SIC (Standard Industrial Classification) codes, financial analyst reports, Hoover's and Moody's reports, *Fortune* rankings, and published articles. We then created a quantitative scoring framework, built around the following six criteria.

BUSINESS FIT: The success-contrast candidate and the fallen company were in similar businesses at the contrast-selection year. In each case, we developed an objective framework for the degree of business overlap, allowing us to score each candidate on a 1-to-4 scale.

SIZE FIT: The success-contrast candidate and the fallen company were of a comparable size at the contrast-selection year.

Score 4: if the revenue ratio is between 0.80 and 1.25

Score 3: if the revenue ratio is between 0.60 and 0.80, or between 1.25 and 1.67

Score 2: if the revenue ratio is between 0.40 and 0.60, or between 1.67 and 2.50

Score 1: if the revenue ratio is under 0.40 or above 2.50

AGE FIT: The success-contrast candidate and the fallen company were of a comparable age at the contrast-selection year.

Score 4: if both the fallen company and the success-contrast candidate were founded before 1950 or if the age ratio is between 0.90 and 1.11

Score 3: if the age ratio is between 0.75 and 0.90, or between 1.11 and 1.33

Score 2: if the age ratio is between 0.50 and 0.75, or between 1.33 and 2.00

Score 1: if the age ratio is below 0.50 or above 2.00

PERFORMANCE FIT: The success-contrast candidate and the fallen company had comparable stock returns in the ten years preceding the contrast-selection year.

Score 4: if there's a 0- to 10-percent difference in cumulative stock returns

Score 3: if there's a 10- to 25-percent difference in cumulative stock returns

Score 2: if there's a 25- to 50-percent difference in cumulative stock returns

Score 1: if there's a 50-percent or greater difference in cumulative stock returns

PERFORMANCE DIVERGENCE: The success-contrast candidate substantially outperformed the fallen company from the contrast-selection year to ten years out.

Score 4: if the ratio of cumulative stock returns of the success-contrast candidate to the fallen company is above 3.0

Score 3: if the ratio of cumulative stock returns of the success-contrast candidate to the fallen company is between 2.0 and 3.0

Score 2: if the ratio of cumulative stock returns of the success-contrast candidate to the fallen company is between 1.5 and 2.0

Score 1: if the ratio of cumulative stock returns of the success-contrast candidate to the fallen company is between 1.0 and 1.5

Automatically exclude the company: if the ratio of cumulative stock returns of the success-contrast candidate to the fallen company is below 1.0

GREATNESS TEST: The success-contrast candidate performed strongly from the contrast-selection year to ten years out and had a strong corporate reputation. Scoring starts with 4 points.

No deduction: if the ratio of its cumulative stock returns to the general market is above 2.5

Deduct 0.5: if the ratio of its cumulative stock returns to the general market is between 2.0 and 2.5

Deduct 1.0: if the ratio of its cumulative stock returns to the general market is between 1.5 and 2.0

Deduct 1.5: if the ratio of its cumulative stock returns to the general market is between 1.0 and 1.5

Deduct 2.0: if the ratio of its cumulative stock returns to the general market is between 0.80 and 1.0

Automatically exclude the company: if the ratio of its cumulative stock returns to the general market is below 0.80

If the company's industry rank on *Fortune*'s "Most Admired Companies" list at the contrast-selection year plus ten years out is:

#1, no deduction

#2 or #3, deduct 0.5

#4 or below, deduct 1.0

Circuit City Success-Contrast Candidate Scoring

Best Buy	18.5
Wal-Mart	14.0
Radio Shack	11.0

HP Success-Contrast Candidate Scoring

IBM	15.5*
Texas Instruments	15.5*
Dell	13.5
Apple	11.0
Intel	10.5
Sun Microsystems	9.5

* IBM wins in the business-fit tiebreaker.

Merck Success-Contrast Candidate Scoring

Johnson & Johnson	19.0
Pfizer	17.0
Abbott Labs	16.0
Eli Lilly	16.0
Wyeth	15.5
Schering-Plough	14.0

Motorola Success-Contrast Candidate Scoring

Texas Instruments	17.5
IBM	15.0
GE	14.5
Intel	14.5
Harris	14.0
Applied Materials	11.0
Cisco	11.0
Emerson	10.5

We were able to identify a strong success-contrast company for each fallen company except for Rubbermaid. In the case of Rubbermaid, we began with twenty-six possibilities. After eliminating companies for lack of business overlap, loss of independence during the time of study, lack of publicly available performance information due to being privately held, or poor performance, we found no company that qualified as a viable success-contrast. The final study set of success-contrast cases appears below. It is interesting to note that the success contrast for one company (Motorola in contrast to Zenith during the 1970s) became a fallen company in the 1990s. There are no guarantees of lasting success!

Fallen Company	Success Contrast
A&P	Kroger
Addressograph	Pitney Bowes
Ames	Wal-Mart
Bank of America	Wells Fargo
Circuit City	Best Buy
HP	IBM
Merck	Johnson & Johnson
Motorola	Texas Instruments
Rubbermaid	None qualified
Scott Paper	Kimberly-Clark
Zenith	Motorola

APPENDIX 3:

FANNIE MAE AND THE

FINANCIAL CRISIS OF 2008

We featured Fannie Mae in *Good to Great* due to its extraordinary performance leap in the early 1980s under David Maxwell. Under Maxwell's leadership, Fannie Mae transformed itself from a bureaucratic, government-chartered entity into a high-powered capital markets enterprise, generating cumulative stock returns substantially above the general stock market. The thirty-year cumulative stock-return pattern used as the basis for selecting Fannie Mae for *Good to Great* ran from 1969 to 1999, and our research regarding Fannie Mae focused on those years.

Unfortunately, Fannie Mae of the 2000s exemplified just the opposite: great to good to nearly gone. As I mentioned earlier in the text, we didn't include Fannie Mae in the full analysis for *How the Mighty Fall* for the simple reason that when we selected our study set of fallen companies in 2005, Fannie Mae (and other financial institutions in our database) hadn't yet fallen, so they didn't qualify for this study. Instead of throwing Fannie Mae into the research project at the last minute because it happened to be in the news, I've decided to include a brief commentary about it in this appendix.

In reviewing the demise of Fannie Mae and other financial institutions in 2008, I kept thinking about a scene from the movie *Titanic*. In that scene, J. Bruce Ismay of the White Star Line, which owned the *Titanic,* turns incredulous when confronted with the impending doom of the giant ship: "But this ship can't sink."

"She's made of iron, sir," replies ship designer Thomas Andrews. "I assure you, she can."

As the housing bubble burst, financial executives at major institutions turned incredulous, seemingly unable to believe the terrifying reality of their situation. In examining the materials we assembled on the demise of Fannie Mae, we found little evidence that the company's executives seriously considered the possibility of failure. Yet in September 2008, Fannie Mae found itself under government conservatorship, a legal status similar to bankruptcy.[172] On October 31, Fannie Mae's stock price, which had stood at $57 a year earlier, had essentially evaporated, falling 98 percent to 93 *cents*.[173]

According to an article in the *New York Times*, Fannie Mae's CEO later defended the company, pointing out that "almost no one expected what was coming. It's not fair to blame us for not predicting the unthinkable."[174] And indeed, nearly every major financial institution got mauled in the housing-bubble, subprime-mortgage mess of 2008, including Fannie Mae's fraternal twin, Freddie Mac, along with institutions like Citigroup. When Vikram Pandit, CEO of Citigroup, appeared on the *Charlie Rose* show in late November 2008, he made the same argument. "How many times have you seen AAA bonds go to zero?" he asked rhetorically, adding that risk-management models simply didn't account for the scenarios that had actually unfolded. He later added, "I'm not so sure anybody . . . *anybody* . . . ran a stress test of the kind of environment that we're living through today." [175]

So, perhaps Fannie Mae just got hammered down by an industry catastrophe; maybe its failure had nothing to do with its self-management. That said, we did find evidence of the first three stages of decline (Stage 1: Hubris Born of Success; Stage 2: Undisciplined Pursuit of More; and Stage 3: Denial of Risk and Peril) at Fannie Mae in the 2000s, leading up to the 2008 crisis.

Maxwell had cultivated an ethic of willful humility while leading Fannie Mae during the 1980s. However, by the early 2000s, Fannie Mae had acquired a reputation for arrogance, enabled by both its extraordinary success and its sense of missionary righteousness vis-à-vis its special role in advancing the American Dream of home ownership. [176] Fannie Mae had long prided itself on being a disciplined organization, especially in managing risk, but it also experienced substantial pressures for growth—from within and from Wall Street—compounded by political pressures to help more low-income families become homeowners. [177] Its 2001 annual report stated that Fannie Mae was on track to double operating earnings per share in the five years ending in 2003, which implied a 15-percent annual growth rate (compared to the 7- to 10-percent growth rate of the overall residential mortgage market at the time). [178] Fannie Mae achieved its goal, appearing headed toward further growth and success, and then became ensnared in an accounting storm. [179]

In September 2004, the Office of Federal Housing Enterprise Oversight (OFHEO) issued a report accusing Fannie Mae of misapplying Generally Accepted Accounting Principles in an effort to minimize earnings volatility.[180] Fannie Mae eventually resolved the crisis, but at a cost. In the words of its 2006 annual report:

"We entered into comprehensive settlements that resolved open matters with the OFHEO special examination, as well as with the SEC's [Security and Exchange Commission's] related investigation. As part of the OFHEO settlement, we agreed to OFHEO's issuance of a consent order. In entering into this settlement, we neither admitted nor denied any wrongdoing or any asserted or implied finding or other basis for the consent order. We also agreed to pay a $400 million civil penalty, with $50 million payable to the U.S. Treasury and $350 million payable to the SEC for distribution to certain shareholders pursuant to the Fair Funds for Investors provision of the Sarbanes-Oxley Act of 2002." [181]

More costly than the financial penalties, Fannie Mae had lost much of its momentum while embroiled in the investigation.

The wounded mortgage giant emerged from the accounting settlement to find a growing housing bubble and aggressive competition from companies like Countrywide, Lehman Brothers, Bear Stearns, and others.[182] Fannie Mae increased its activity in subprime mortgages, although not to the extent of some other companies.[183] As a Fannie Mae executive said to the *New York Times*, "Everybody understood that we were now buying loans that we would have previously rejected, and that the models were telling us that we were charging way too little. But our mandate was to stay relevant and to serve low-income bor-

rowers. So that's what we did." [184] As the housing bubble rup-
tured, Fannie Mae posted losses of $2.2 billion in the first quarter
of 2008 and $2.3 billion in the second quarter. To help stave off a
collapse of the entire U.S. financial system, the U.S. government
put Fannie Mae and Freddie Mac into conservatorship, with the
aim of restructuring them by 2010.[185]

Here are a few observations and lessons:

- Financial institutions have a peculiar relationship relative to Stages 3, 4, and 5. Because of the high levels of
  leverage that financial enterprises often use, a relatively
  small set of losses can create a potentially catastrophic
  loss. Financial institutions caught in a risk-gone-bad
  downward spiral can crash downward from Stage 3
  right into Stage 5, sinking so fast that there remains
  little time to grasp for salvation.

- Companies already in the stages of decline are ex-
  tremely vulnerable to turbulence. If the financial storm
  of 2008 had never happened, or if it hadn't become so
  severe, perhaps Fannie Mae would have had an opportunity to reverse its own decline and return to greatness by its own efforts. It lost that opportunity in the
  calamity of September 2008.

- I'm struck by how the stages of decline—Hubris Born
  of Success, Undisciplined Pursuit of More, Denial of
  Risk and Peril, Grasping for Salvation (Government,
  save us!), and finally, Capitulation to Irrelevance or
  Death—map fairly well not just to individual companies, but perhaps even to an entire industry, such as financial services or the American auto industry. Even

so, it is worth pointing out that companies need not be imprisoned by their industries. Not every financial company toppled during the 2008 crisis, and some seized the opportunity to take advantage of weaker competitors in the midst of the tumult.

- Finally, there's a provocative lesson: beware the hubris that can arise in conjunction with missionary zeal. In the *Built to Last* study, Jerry Porras and I found that enduring great companies passionately adhere to a set of timeless core values and pursue a core purpose beyond just making money. But there is also a risk to manage: having an almost righteous sense of one's values and purpose ("We're the good guys") can perhaps make a company more vulnerable to Stages 1 to 3. Fannie Mae's missionary zeal for expanding the American Dream of home ownership to as many Americans as possible contributed, in part, to its arrogance, its pursuit of growth, and even its increased risk profile. Whenever people begin to confuse the nobility of their cause with the goodness and wisdom of their actions—"We're good people in pursuit of a noble cause, and therefore our decisions are good and wise"—they can perhaps more easily lead themselves astray. Bad decisions made with good intentions are still bad decisions.

APPENDIX 4.A:

EVIDENCE TABLE—SUBVERTING THE COMPLACENCY HYPOTHESIS

Note: This table is designed to show that great companies can fall even if engaged in energetic and ambitious activity, thereby undermining the hypothesis that all great companies fall because they become complacent. In fact, as this table illustrates, ten of the eleven great companies in our analysis fell despite showing behaviors contrary to complacency.

Addressograph, Stage 2: 1956–1971

- Highly cognizant of the threat from Xerox, merged with Charles Bruning Co. to better compete. Launched the Bruning 3000, but the product failed.[186]
- Developed a duplicator + copier (AMCD-I), but the product never made it to market because it lacked two-sided capability, encountered production snags, and faced competition from other internal products.
- Launched a crash program to develop new products, releasing twenty-three new products in three years.[187]

Ames, Stage 2: 1982–1988

- Grew by making a series of significant acquisitions.
- Moved aggressively from a rural focus to a more urban focus.[188]
- Embarked upon experimental ventures in stationery, variety, and craft and hobby stores.
- Acquired Zayre department stores, with anticipation to more than double the size of the company.
- Multiplied sales five times in five-year period ranging from 1983 to 1988.[189]

Bank of America, Stage 2: 1970–1979

- Made a huge push internationally. In the 1960s, moved from having fewer than 20 to more than 90 international branches, then from 1971 to 1977, increased assets in overseas branches and subsidiaries by more than three times. Decentralized authority for international lending so as to increase entrepreneurial growth in foreign markets.[190]
- Committed to action, CEO A. W. Clausen stated, "Our keyword must be 'action.' . . . Our mistakes must be the mistakes of *decision,* not the worse mistakes of indecision itself." [191]
- Launched a venture capital partnership for high-risk, direct investments in small technology companies.[192]
- Doubled total assets from 1970 to 1974, then nearly doubled them again from 1974 to 1979.[193]
- Transformed BankAmericard (which it invented) into the ubiquitous Visa card.[194]
- In the late 1970s, significantly increased fixed-rate mortgages, agricultural lending, construction lending, and loans to high-risk countries in Latin America and Africa.[195]

Circuit City, Stage 2: 1992–1997

- Made significant commitments for growth. Stated in 1996 that it aimed to more than double revenue to $15 billion by 2000. Anticipated growing to 800 Circuit City Superstores by 2000, an 80 percent increase over 1997.[196]
- Multiplied revenue 2.7X (from $2.8 billion to $7.7 billion) in five-year period from 1992 to 1997, with an average growth rate of 22 percent per year.

• Committed to building CarMax as an exciting new business. By 1997, CarMax had grown from zero to $510 million in revenue. Issued $412 million equity in 1997 to fund growth, with the goal of expanding to more than 80 CarMax stores by 2002.[197]

• Began development of Divx, a new home video technology that would allow for a no-return, rental-like system for home movie viewing.[198]

HP, Stage 2: 1992–1997

• Multiplied revenue 2.6X (from $16.4 billion to $42.9 billion) in five-year period from 1992 to 1997, resulting in faster average growth than that achieved in the 25-year period from 1966 to 1991.[199]

• Accelerated new product development. By 1993, 70 percent of HP's orders came from products introduced in the previous two years, up from 30 percent a decade earlier.[200]

• In 1996, picked as the "Best Performing Company" in America by *Forbes,* edging out GE, Johnson & Johnson, and Intel. The article was titled, "Top Corporate Performance 1995: 'Boy Scouts on a Rampage.'"[201]

• CEO Lew Platt waged war on complacency and built HP for innovation. "Fear of complacency is what keeps me awake at night," he said. "You must anticipate that whatever made you successful in the past won't in the future." Platt believed that the best defense was preemptive self-destruction and renewal. "It's counter to human nature, but you have to kill your business while it is still working," he said. "My job is to maintain an environment that encourages healthy paranoia."[202]

• Dominated the printer industry with an Intel-like cycle of brutalizing competitors: come out with the next generation of better products just as your competitors catch up to your current generation, devastate your competitors with ferocious pricing, and then repeat the cycle, fast. Applied this model to personal computers and moved from #11 to #3 in four years.[203]

• Made a significant move into e-commerce by buying Verifone.[204] Advanced the concept of an "information utility" to link digital devices with the ease of plugging appliances into a wall and moved into digital photography.[205]

Merck, Stage 2: 1993–1998

• In 1993, acquired Medco Containment Services, Inc., for $6 billion (on a 1992 revenue base of $9.7 billion). Medco was acquired to control distribution in profit-hostile environment.[206]

• Established #1 business objective as being a top-tier growth company. Planned to achieve growth by investing in fundamental R&D for potential breakthrough drugs, achieving the full potential of managed pharmaceutical care, and preserving the profitability of the core pharmaceutical business.[207]

• Maintained scientific advancement, on track to patenting more new compounds than any other pharmaceutical company.[208]

• Instituted significant organizational change, creating "worldwide business strategy teams," each focused on key diseases, to drive product and market development.[209]

Motorola, Stage 2: 1990–1995

• Sought to double in size every five years.[210] From 1990 to 1995, grew revenue from $11 billion to $27 billion.

• Positioned itself strongly for trends: wireless, cellular, electronics, and globalization, with farsighted investments made in China (by 1996, had the largest stake in China of any U.S. company).[211]

• Took Iridium satellite-communications project into full development (spun it into separate LLC in 1991).[212]

• Made major bet on PowerPC microprocessor (in partnership with IBM and Apple) to challenge Intel.[213]

• Demonstrated high levels of innovation, increasing its patents from 613 in 1991 to 1,016 in 1995.[214]

• Heralded as "The Company that Likes to Obsolete Itself."[215]

• Pioneered Six Sigma quality, one of the first companies to pursue 3.4 defects per million in its products.[216]

• Encouraged a combative "cult of conflict" to ensure that the best technology and market ideas won.[217]

Rubbermaid, Stage 2: 1980–1993

• Increased revenues more than six times and earnings nearly fifteen times from 1980 to 1993, at one point generating forty consecutive quarters of earnings growth.[218]

• Created an innovation machine. By 1991, generated more than 30 percent of its revenue from products introduced in the previous five years.[219] In 1992, introduced on average one new product every day, 365 days a year.[220]

• In the early 1990s, aimed to add one new market segment every 12 to 18 months.[221]

• Cultivated an intense drive for growth and self-reinvention. "We have to reinvent ourselves continuously."[222] "Our major growth objective is to double our sales, earnings, and earnings per share every five years."[223]

Scott Paper, Stage 2: 1962–1970

• Instituted diversification program to fuel new growth. Bought a textbook paper manufacturer, plastic-coating company, and company that made teacher training kits for K–12 education. Launched a disposable-products company, with creative ideas like disposable paper dresses and graduation gowns. Made a move into resorts and poolside/patio furniture.[224]

• Adopted a brand management model, with brand managers responsible for their own products' earnings and for their own research, manufacturing, advertising, and sales—a significant change from the previous approach.

• At the same time, Scott did not respond aggressively to the threat from P&G during the early 1960s (some evidence indicates that it had a "genteel" culture that lacked a fighting spirit).[225]

Zenith, Stage 2: 1966–1974

• Achieved ambition to become #1 in U.S. black-and-white television market by 1959.[226]

• Achieved ambition to overtake RCA to become #1 in color televisions by 1972.[227]

• Made a big bet on the visionary idea of pay TV. Didn't succeed, largely because Zenith was nearly two decades ahead of its time.[228]

• From 1970 to 1973, invested in significant capacity expansion, with new plants in Taiwan, Hong Kong, along the Mexican border, and elsewhere.[229]

• Poured money into automating plants in the United States as way to compete in tough global economic conditions.[230]

• Developed a reputation for being a fast follower in new technologies; once a new approach had been proven, would aggressively adopt it.[231]

Cases Demonstrating Significant Complacency
A&P, Stage 2: 1958–1963

- Became known as the "Hermit Kingdom," with a reputation for isolation and resistance to any change. "You can't quarrel with a hundred years of success" became a common internal refrain.[232]
- Forty percent of founder stock allocated to Hartford Foundation, which demanded high dividends. From 1958 to 1962, turned record-high profits into record-high dividends, paying out more than 90 percent in dividends.[233]
- Invested less in new stores than competitors. In 1962, "with 33 percent of the volume and 36 percent of the total number of stores, expended only 18 percent of the capital investments in stores made by the top ten chains."[234]
- Allowed stores to fall into disrepair. Stuck with an outdated store format, while competitors began investing in larger store formats that would eventually become superstores.[235]

APPENDIX 4.B:

EVIDENCE TABLE—GRASPING FOR SALVATION

A&P

Falling in the early 1970s, set off an industry price war—what one industry competitor called "a desperation effort that is throwing the industry into chaos"—converting more than four thousand A&P stores to a new format called WEO (short for "Where Economy Originates") and driving prices below costs to regain market share.[236] Hired a charismatic savior CEO from the outside. Bet on a new division of "Family Mart" combination stores, selling everything from televisions to bread, milk, and beer. Launched new advertising and image-making campaigns. After a brief return to profitability, fell into a string of losses, which further eroded the balance sheet. Lurched for other saviors, including an investment from a German company and yet another outside CEO.[237]

Addressograph

In the early 1970s, experienced significant decline in profits due to product failures and lured an outside CEO from Honeywell with a large cash signing bonus and stock grant who failed to reverse the decline. Turned to another charismatic outsider who threw the company into a traumatic re-invention. Pinned hopes on a savior strategy, leaping into the Office of the Future. (The strategy, according to an Addressograph executive just a few years later, was "to leapfrog from where [Addressograph] was in the mid-1970s to maybe 15 years into the future. The leap did not go as planned."[238]

Ames

After the Zayre acquisition, fell into bankruptcy protection. New CEO brought in a team of hired guns to save the company. Emerged from bankruptcy with yet another new CEO in place, who wrote in his first annual report, "Prior to and during Chapter 11, Ames attempted various merchandising and marketing strategies that may have confused many traditional Ames customers." Within two years, brought in yet another CEO, who began a "fundamental transformation" of the company, changing strategy again, this time to "opportunistic purchasing and micro-marketing," deemphasizing the everyday-low-price model in favor of focusing on being in stock and putting in place new flashy programs with taglines like "55 Gold" and "Bargains by the Bagful." In 1998, embarked on the acquisition of Hills Department Stores, nearly doubling the size of the company overnight. Liquidated less than four years later.[239]

Bank of America

In the mid-1980s, began to visibly tumble. Made extensive use of external culture consultants, putting almost 2,000 employees through what *Fortune* called "a series of corporate encounter groups." *Banker Magazine* reported that the "wide-ranging programme . . . involves a total revision of its philosophy, tactics, strategy and regional priorities." Launched a $5 billion program in new technology to rush into the Information Age. Cut the dividend for the first time in more than five decades. CEO resigned and the board brought a former CEO back out of retirement to save the company; he then brought in former Wells Fargo officers to help turn things around.[240]

Circuit City

Facing declining revenue in 2002, launched a new logo and program tagged "We're with you" with a major advertising campaign. In early 2003, made a drastic move to eliminate commissioned sales; terminated more than 3,000 experienced, higher-paid salespeople in favor of less-experienced, lower-cost, hourly people. Replaced "sales counselors" with "product specialists." Posted losses in 2003 and 2004. Launched new branding campaign in 2004 under the tagline "Just What I Needed" and yet another new brand dubbed "Firedog" in 2006. Hired an executive from Best Buy who became president in 2005 and CEO in 2006. In 2008, considered a potential sale to salvage something for its shareholders, only to see a bid from Blockbuster evaporate.[241]

HP

In the late 1980s, appeared to be falling behind relative to the technology bubble and began to perform below Wall Street expectations. CEO resigned and the board hired a high-profile, charismatic leader from the outside. Launched a radical cultural and strategic transformation, built around the Internet. Then in 2001, bid to buy Compaq Computer at a cost of approximately $24 billion, advancing its case with dramatic rhetoric: the "best and fastest way to increase the value" . . . "in one move, we dramatically improve" . . . "enable us to quickly address" . . . "we immediately double" . . . "in a single strategic move" . . . "will allow HP to accelerate" . . . "will transform our industry" . . . and so on. Earnings became erratic. In early 2005, the board fired its CEO and hired a replacement from the outside.[242]

Merck

Never reached Stage 4.

Motorola

Upon falling into visible decline in the late 1990s, bet on "harnessing the power of wireless broadband and the Internet"—right at the height of the telecom and dot-com boom. Later admitted that "like others, we inopportunely chased the dot-com and telecom boom." Aimed to recast itself from being a hardware-oriented to a software-oriented company. Made a $17 billion acquisition of General Instruments. Undertook radical cultural and strategic change; "Everything has been modified or changed at the company." Bet on a new program called "Intelligence Everywhere." Began researching a move into biotechnology. Overhauled the wireless business three times in four years. In late 2003, hired a savior CEO from the outside who lasted fewer than four years.[243]

Rubbermaid

In the fourth quarter of 1995, not long after appearing as the #1 "Most Admired Company" in America, reported a loss. Announced its first major restructuring, cutting nearly six thousand product variations, closing nine plants, and eliminating 1,170 jobs.[244] At the same time, made one of the largest acquisitions in its history. Announced the sale of its office-products business, reversing a strategic imperative set just a few years earlier. Launched a radical marketing bet on the Internet as "a renaissance tool," yet profits dropped again, triggering a second major restructuring. Launched the biggest new marketing campaign in its history. Recast incentive compensation, with stronger links to its stock price. Made another big acquisition to quadruple European sales. Lost its independence to Newell Corporation in 1998.[245]

Scott Paper

From 1981 to 1988, embarked on a dramatic turnaround, a revolutionary transformation designed to shock the company out of its stupor. Instituted more pervasive incentive pay. Put hundreds of managers through retreats to imbue them with a new mindset, making the company "dynamically reborn."[246] Hired strategy consultants to help reshape direction.[247] Initial results looked good, but then profits dropped. Fell into restructuring doom loop, with $167 million in restructuring charges in 1990, followed by a $249 million restructuring charge in 1991, followed by another $490 million restructuring charge in early 1994, totaling nearly $1 billion.[248] Brought in a fix-it CEO from the outside who slashed jobs, cut costs, and sold the company to archrival Kimberly-Clark.

Zenith

In 1977, posted its first loss in decades. CEO resigned. Leapt after a whole bunch of new opportunities at the same time. "If we have any plan at all, it's that we'll take a shot at everything," said a Zenith senior leader. Over a three-year period, moved into VCRs, videodiscs, telephones that linked through televisions, home-security video cameras, cable TV decoders, and personal computers (via the acquisition of the computer company Heath). To fund all these moves, doubled its debt-to-equity ratio.[249]

APPENDIX 5:

WHAT MAKES FOR THE
"RIGHT PEOPLE" IN KEY SEATS?

While the specifics regarding who would be the right people for key seats vary across organizations, our research yields six generic characteristics:

1. **THE RIGHT PEOPLE FIT WITH THE COMPANY'S CORE VALUES.** Great companies build almost cult-like cultures, where those who do not share the institution's values find themselves surrounded by antibodies and ejected like a virus. People often ask, "How do we get people to share our core values?" The answer: you don't. You hire people who already have a predisposition to your core values, and hang on to them.

2. **THE RIGHT PEOPLE DON'T NEED TO BE TIGHTLY MANAGED.** The moment you feel the need to tightly manage someone, you might have made a hiring mistake. If you have the

right people, you don't need to spend a lot of time "motivating" or "managing" them. They'll be productively neurotic, *self*-motivated and *self*-disciplined, compulsively driven to do the best they can because it's simply part of their DNA.

3. **THE RIGHT PEOPLE UNDERSTAND THAT THEY DO NOT HAVE "JOBS"; THEY HAVE RESPONSIBILITIES.** They grasp the difference between their task list and their true *responsibilities*. The right people can complete the statement, "I am the one person ultimately responsible for . . ."

4. **THE RIGHT PEOPLE FULFILL THEIR COMMITMENTS.** In a culture of discipline, people view commitments as sacred—they do what they say, without complaint. Equally, this means that they take great care in saying what they will do, careful to never overcommit or to promise what they cannot deliver.

5. **THE RIGHT PEOPLE ARE PASSIONATE ABOUT THE COMPANY AND ITS WORK.** Nothing great happens without passion, and the right people display remarkable intensity.

6. **THE RIGHT PEOPLE DISPLAY "WINDOW AND MIRROR" MATURITY.** When things go well, the right people point out the window, giving credit to factors other than themselves; they shine a light on other people who contributed to the success and take little credit themselves. Yet when things go awry, they do not blame circumstances or other people for setbacks and failures; they point in the mirror and say, "I'm responsible."

APPENDIX 6.A:

DECLINE AND RECOVERY CASE

IBM

IBM's Rebound Under Louis V. Gerstner, Jr.

Ratio of Cumulative Stock Returns to General Market
Gerstner becomes CEO in 1993 and retires at start of 2003

SYNOPSIS: IBM grew to become one of the most admired and successful corporations of the twentieth century under the leadership of Thomas J. Watson, Sr., and Thomas J. Watson, Jr.; they led IBM for a total of fifty-seven years (1914–1956 for Watson Sr. and 1956–1971 for Watson Jr.). IBM became a dominant force in computing, making huge leaps with programs like the IBM 360 project. From 1926 to 1972, IBM beat the general stock market by more than seventy times; a $1,000 investment in IBM in 1926 would have returned more than $5 million by 1972. In the mid-1980s, however, IBM began a steady slide and then plummeted in the early 1990s, posting its first losses in more than seven decades, losing more than $15 billion from 1991 to 1993. In 1993, the board hired Lou Gerstner as CEO, who turned IBM around and then set the foundations for IBM to become a great company once again.[250]

I've outlined IBM's recovery through the lens of the good-to-great concepts below. (For an explanation of these concepts, see Appendix 7.)

LEVEL 5 LEADERSHIP: Gerstner came in as a savior CEO yet clearly had the discipline to make difficult decisions (and to resist making panicky decisions). While it is not entirely clear if Gerstner began his IBM tenure as a Level 5 leader, he grew to have a Level 5 passion for the company, noting at the end of his tenure that he "fell in love with IBM." He dedicated his book, *Who Says Elephants Can't Dance?* "to the thousands of IBMers who never gave up on their company, their colleagues, and themselves. They are the real heroes of the reinvention of IBM." In the end, Gerstner was clearly ambitious for IBM first and foremost, beyond himself.[251]

FIRST WHO, THEN WHAT: Gerstner first focused on rebuilding his team, describing his focus on getting the right people in key seats as "my top priority during those first few weeks." He retooled the compensation system so that he would not lose any key people. He rebuilt the team around himself with people he knew he could trust—a new communications executive, a new head of corporate marketing, a new CFO, a new general manager of the personal computer division—and removed executives who did not share his sense of urgency or who failed to deliver on their responsibilities.[252]

CONFRONT THE BRUTAL FACTS: Gerstner believed that assessing the brutal facts—where IBM was failing, where IBM couldn't be excellent, why IBM was losing market share, how IBM's cost structure had become bloated, what IBM's critical customers *really* thought, how the competition had come to see IBM as irrelevant, and so forth—however hard that might be, preceded developing a vision. "If the last thing IBM needed in July 1993 was a vision, the second last thing it needed was for me [Gerstner] to stand up and say that IBM had basically everything right." Gerstner and his team met with customers to get candid feedback, kicking off a transition to return IBM once again to being an externally focused, customer-driven enterprise. They confronted the fact that IBM had been milking the mainframe business by keeping prices high and losing market share. (The Gerstner team dramatically lowered the price per unit of mainframe processing power by 96 percent over the next seven years.) They confronted the fact that IBM had to cut $7 billion in costs in order to survive. They confronted the fact that OS/2 had failed and Windows had won. They confronted the fact that

IBM faced competition more threatening than it had faced for most of its history.[253]

HEDGEHOG CONCEPT: The cornerstone of IBM's transition rested on one central idea: an obsessive passion for the customer would be at the center of IBM's universe. This shift then led to a crucial insight—customers desperately needed someone to integrate all the disparate pieces of information technology, individually tailored to solve their specific problems, into a single package, and this need would grow as technological change and the shift to networked computing accelerated. From this came the essence of IBM's hedgehog concept: IBM could be the best in the world at technology-integration services. "The idea that all this complicated, difficult-to-integrate, proprietary collection of technologies was going to be purchased by customers who would be willing to be their own general contractors made no sense."[254]

CULTURE OF DISCIPLINE: Gerstner exemplified the principle of turning a culture of bureaucracy into a culture of discipline, one in which people had freedom within a framework of demanding performance standards, values, and accountability. "'Respect for the individual' had devolved to . . . a culture of entitlement, where 'the individual' didn't have to do anything to *earn* respect—he or she expected rich benefits and lifetime employment simply by virtue of having been hired." He laid out a framework of eight principles of IBM performance, and any business leader who failed to deliver results consistent with this framework would no longer hold a position of significant responsibility. The Gerstner team maintained focus on the hedgehog concept, noting "a good portion of our success was due to all of the deals we *didn't* do."[255]

FLYWHEEL, NOT DOOM LOOP: Gerstner resisted reactive moves, taking time to rigorously analyze IBM's problems. Despite the general view held by analysts, the press, and other experts that IBM needed to be broken into pieces, Gerstner chose to keep the company together. He unplugged activities that did not fit with the hedgehog concept: stopped OS/2, stopped developing applications software, and sold the Federal Systems division. He kept a low profile with the media, never allowing hype to precede results; he engaged in the disciplined practice of underpromising and overdelivering. He turned away big acquisitions that did not fit with the strategy or that would fail to deliver significant profit. As IBM's integration-services concept gained traction, the Gerstner team capitalized on the rise of the Internet and shift to networked computing to launch IBM e-services.[256]

CLOCK BUILDING, NOT TIME TELLING: Gerstner wrote, "I came to see, in my time at IBM, that culture isn't just one aspect of the game— it *is* the game." To reinforce the idea that executives were responsible for creating value rather than simply being entitled to wealth, executives would no longer receive stock options unless they concurrently bought IBM stock with their own cash. Gerstner constructed a senior leadership group capped at 300 people. There was no year-to-year tenure on the group; every year, Gerstner reconstituted the group based on each member's performance; only 71 of the original 300 remained in the senior leadership group in 2002. Gerstner engaged in rigorous succession planning for the next CEO.[257]

PRESERVE THE CORE/STIMULATE PROGRESS: Gerstner unraveled the mix-up between core values and operating practices. He overturned hidebound traditions and stupid rules, while simultaneously revitalizing IBM's core values and semi-neurotic passion for excellence and success—"You're *IBM*, damn it!" He set the audacious goal to build the largest, most influential information technology-services enterprise in the world, betting heavily on the insight that networked computing would replace distributed computing; from this, he launched e-business as IBM's "moon shot" in the 1990s and early 2000s. The Gerstner team reengineered almost all aspects of business processes, removing more than $14 billion in inefficiencies from 1993 to 2002.[258]

APPENDIX 6.B:

DECLINE AND RECOVERY CASE

NUCOR

Nucor's Rebound Under Daniel R. DiMicco
Ratio of Cumulative Stock Returns to General Market
DiMicco becomes CEO in 2000

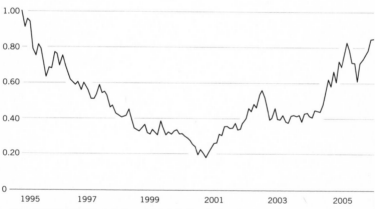

SYNOPSIS: Nucor earned a position as one of the most remarkable good-to-great cases in the last fifty years. Facing possible bankruptcy in 1965, the board turned the company over to Ken Iverson. Under Iverson, Nucor built its first steel mills because it could not find a reliable supplier. Nucor people discovered that they had a knack for making steel better and cheaper than anyone else, so they built additional mini-mills. Nucor eventually generated greater profits than any other steel company on the Fortune 1000 list. From 1975 to 1990, its stock outperformed the general stock market by more than five times. The cornerstone of the company's success was its marrying a performance-oriented culture with advanced steel-making technology, which steadily drove down the cost per finished ton of steel. In the mid-1990s, Nucor began to falter during a period of executive turmoil at the end of Iverson's career. He retired in 1996 after a messy boardroom showdown, and his chosen CEO successor resigned in 1999. In 2000, the board put longtime insider Daniel DiMicco into the CEO role and Nucor regained its footing; its stock performance once again took on a beat-the-market trajectory, and Nucor proceeded to have the most profitable years in its history.[259]

I've outlined Nucor's recovery through the lens of the good-to-great concepts below. (For an explanation of these concepts, see Appendix 7.)

LEVEL 5 LEADERSHIP: DiMicco displayed long-term dedication to Nucor and its culture, having joined the company in 1982, eighteen years before becoming CEO.[260] He maintained Nucor's egalitarian, no-class-status culture, flying commercial, taking phone calls from all employees, making more coffee when he poured the last cup, and operating out of a drab, cheap-looking headquarters in a strip-mall-style, low-rise office building. DiMicco continued to cultivate a culture in which management was in service to employees, not the other way around.[261] He practiced giving credit to others and taking little credit for himself. Despite the executive turmoil associated with the end of the Iverson era, DiMicco highlighted the debt he owed to his predecessors: "Who we are today is the culmination of the efforts and the dedication of our leadership—in particular, Ken Iverson and his team."[262]

FIRST WHO, THEN WHAT: DiMicco continued the tradition of putting every employee's name—all 18,000 of them in 2007—on the cover of the annual report, reflecting the idea that Nucor's strength was based first and foremost on having the right type of people who fit with the Nucor culture. DiMicco and his team retained the philosophy that it is better to hire people with the right work ethic and character and teach them how to make steel than to hire people who know how to make steel but lack the Nucor work ethic and character traits. Under DiMicco, Nucor increased attention to developing, rather than just selecting, the right people, creating customized leadership-development programs for each and every manager.[263]

CONFRONT THE BRUTAL FACTS: DiMicco and his team confronted the rising threat of Chinese steel and paid increased attention to the risks of facing unfair trading practices.[264] They confronted the risks associated with volatile energy prices and created a hedging strategy for its natural gas purchases.[265] They employed conservative financial accounting practices and maintained a strong balance sheet to be able to weather storms and seize opportunities to gain market share over weaker competitors in difficult times.[266]

HEDGEHOG CONCEPT: Nucor built itself on a simple concept: a passionate dedication to taking care of its customers by monomaniacally harnessing culture and technology to produce low-cost steel while steadily increasing profit per ton of finished steel.[267] DiMicco and his team remained committed to this central idea while making appropriate strategic changes (see Preserve the Core/Stimulate Progress below). DiMicco remained relentlessly focused on only those selective arenas in which Nucor could attain best-in-the-world status and superior economic returns, and jettisoned businesses that failed these tests, such as its bearing products and iron-carbide operations.[268]

CULTURE OF DISCIPLINE: DiMicco reinvigorated the intense culture of productivity that defined Nucor. Instead of focusing on employee rank and status, Nucor emphasized performance; those teams that met or exceeded productivity goals without compromising safety or quality received compensation 100 to 200 percent in excess of their hourly wages. Bonuses were based on team and unit performance, which encouraged all employees to assume full responsibility for productivity, not just for their little piece of the puzzle. If a team produced a bad batch of steel, its members would lose their bonuses; if that batch reached the customer, they could lose three times that amount. The entire system was designed to reinforce the idea that no one at Nucor received a paycheck simply by virtue of having a "job"; rather, each employee was responsible for contributing to the dual goals of producing high-quality, low-cost steel and taking care of the customer.[269]

FLYWHEEL, NOT DOOM LOOP: DiMicco did the exact opposite of grasping for salvation and falling into a doom loop of chronic inconsistency. He understood the importance of consistency, building cumulative momentum in the flywheel. In the wake of the tumultuous events of 2001 and the disruptive challenges facing the steel industry, his letter to shareholders that year stated, "I wrote the same thing in my letter to you last year, and I expect you'll be reading it 12 months from now. No matter what's happening to the industry and in the world around us, we must never lose sight of our main goal." And in 2003, after a particularly turbulent time in the steel industry, he wrote, "Whatever turn the economy takes, Nucor will remain true to the principles that have guided us through nearly four decades of uninterrupted profitability and growth."[270]

CLOCK BUILDING, NOT TIME TELLING: The ultimate testament to the Nucor system is the fact that the company survived its tumultuous transition beyond the thirty-year tenure of its guiding genius, Ken Iverson. DiMicco committed to reinvigorating the Nucor culture and organization so that the company's sustained recovery would not depend on his leadership alone.

PRESERVE THE CORE/STIMULATE PROGRESS: DiMicco explicitly embraced the idea of holding values and principles constant, while changing practices and strategies to endlessly adapt to a changing world: "Businesses must evolve while ensuring that core principles are not being compromised."[271] Key mechanisms for driving progress under DiMicco included paying greater attention to taking care of customers, using their demands as a constant catalyst for improvement, and creating an internal benchmarking mechanism.[272] DiMicco changed the longtime practice of relying almost exclusively on internally developed mini-mill sites and added selective acquisitions based on three disciplined decision criteria: don't overpay, stick to businesses you know, and ensure cultural compatibility.[273] He invested in and experimented with new technologies, such as creating the world's first production installation for the direct strip-casting of carbon sheet steel.[274]

APPENDIX 6.C:

DECLINE AND RECOVERY CASE
NORDSTROM

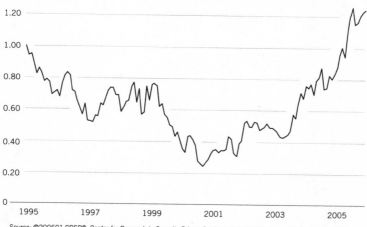

Nordstrom's Rebound Under Blake W. Nordstrom
Ratio of Cumulative Stock Returns to General Market
Nordstrom becomes president in 2000

SYNOPSIS: Known for extraordinary customer service, Nordstrom made its reputation as one of the great retailing companies of the twentieth century. In the 1990s, the company began a long slide and took a dramatic downturn in 2000, with same-store sales actually declining. From 2000 to 2006, Nordstrom strongly recovered when fourth-generation family member Blake Nordstrom assumed leadership and refocused on the primary flywheel that had made the company great in the first place—the customer-service, professional-sales flywheel—while substantially improving background systems, such as inventory controls.[275]

I've outlined Nordstrom's recovery through the lens of the good-to-great concepts below. (For an explanation of these concepts, see Appendix 7.)

LEVEL 5 LEADERSHIP: Blake Nordstrom answered his own phone, as had been Nordstrom family custom. He reestablished the inverted-pyramid structure that placed executives at the bottom, and customers and front-line salespeople at the top. He accepted responsibility for the company's problems: "It was evident to my cousins and me that [our fall] was our fault—not the culture's fault, but us personally."[276]

FIRST WHO, THEN WHAT: Nordstrom's transition began with significant changes in the leadership team—including the CEO, CIO, CFO, and president of full-line stores. The Nordstrom team re-embraced the idea of hiring based on values and character, not skills—"We can hire nice people and teach them to sell, but we can't hire salespeople and teach them to be nice." They returned to the rigor of having the right people in key seats. As one Nordstrom leader put it, "I would rather we lost lawsuits from time to time than keep employees that are not up to our standards. Because a weak employee will make the others around him weak, and drag them down."[277]

CONFRONT THE BRUTAL FACTS: Blake Nordstrom confronted the fact that Nordstrom had strayed from its obsessive culture of customer service and that it badly needed to upgrade its basic systems, in particular through tying inventory systems to point-of-sale systems. He put $200 million into a new perpetual-inventory system so that Nordstrom could both reduce inventory costs and increase the chances that a salesperson could easily locate the exact item a customer desired.[278]

HEDGEHOG CONCEPT: The Nordstrom team rediscovered the company's core concept, that it could be the best department store chain in the world in creating a relationship between the salesperson and the customer. The recovery was based on a simple, elegant idea: get back to building lasting relationships with customers by supporting individual sales professionals with vastly improved background systems (especially inventory systems) and thereby improve core economics measured by return on invested capital. They gained deeper understanding that economic returns were driven by margin dollars divided by average inventory.[279]

CULTURE OF DISCIPLINE: The Nordstrom team returned to the primary approach that had made Nordstrom great in the first place—getting passionate sales professionals, setting very high performance and customer-service expectations, and giving them the freedom to make decisions that would best serve the customer. They retained the Nordstrom rule book, which specified that the only rule is to use good judgment in all situations. "Perhaps the biggest accomplishment," wrote Blake Nordstrom in the 2003 annual report, "is that we are becoming more disciplined as a company."[280]

FLYWHEEL, NOT DOOM LOOP: Blake Nordstrom focused on "small but meaningful steps," not big, dramatic moves. He confronted the failure of the $40 million "Reinvent yourself" campaign: "[It] was an attempt to do something different, and we lost sight of what we are. The customers obviously didn't want to reinvent themselves and didn't want our company to reinvent ourselves." In 2004, Blake Nordstrom wrote, "Success for our company is not going to take a new strategy or an entirely new business model. Instead it's taking what we already do well and continuing to execute those strengths."[281]

CLOCK BUILDING, NOT TIME TELLING: Blake Nordstrom focused on building the culture and supporting systems to enhance the culture so that Nordstrom's recovery would not depend on the presence of any particular leader. He rebuilt his executive team so that the leadership of the company would not depend entirely upon him; if he were to step away, the success of the turnaround would likely continue. At the time of this writing, Blake Nordstrom remains president.[282]

PRESERVE THE CORE/STIMULATE PROGRESS: Blake Nordstrom emphasized reigniting enduring Nordstrom core values (service to the customer above all else, a passion for improvement, entrepre-neurial work ethic, excellence in reputation) yet made dramatic changes in the systems and practices required to actualize those values—new systems, shared best practices, more disciplined buying practices.[283]

APPENDIX 7:

GOOD-TO-GREAT FRAMEWORK—
CONCEPT SUMMARY

Note: At our website, www.jimcollins.com, we have posted a diagnostic tool for assessing an organization through the lens of these concepts. The diagnostic tool is free for use inside any organization.

(The principles in Stages 1 through 3 derive from the research for the book *Good to Great* by Jim Collins; the principles in Stage 4 derive from the book *Built to Last* by Jim Collins and Jerry I. Porras.)

STAGE 1: DISCIPLINED PEOPLE

LEVEL 5 LEADERSHIP: Level 5 leaders are ambitious first and foremost for the cause, the organization, the work—not themselves—and they have the fierce resolve to do whatever

By Applying the Good-to-Great Framework (Inputs of Greatness) →	You Build the Foundations of →	A Great Organization (Outputs of Greatness)
Stage 1: **DISCIPLINED PEOPLE** Level 5 Leadership First Who, Then What		**Delivers Superior Performance** In business, performance is defined by financial returns and achievement of corporate purpose. In the social sectors, performance is defined by results and efficiency in delivering on the social mission.
Stage 2: **DISCIPLINED THOUGHT** Confront the Brutal Facts The Hedgehog Concept		**Makes a Distinctive Impact** The organization makes such a unique contribution to the communities it touches and does its work with such unadulterated excellence that if it were to disappear, it would leave a hole that could not be easily filled by any other institution on the planet.
Stage 3: **DISCIPLINED ACTION** Culture of Discipline The Flywheel		
Stage 4: **BUILDING GREATNESS TO LAST** Clock Building, Not Time Telling Preserve the Core/ Stimulate Progress		**Achieves Lasting Endurance** The organization can deliver exceptional results over a long period of time, beyond any single leader, great idea, market cycle, or well-funded program. When hit with setbacks, it bounces back even stronger than before.

it takes to make good on that ambition. A Level 5 leader displays a paradoxical blend of personal humility and professional will.

FIRST WHO, THEN WHAT: Those who build great organizations make sure they have the right people on the bus, the wrong people off the bus, and the right people in the key seats *before* they figure out where to drive the bus. They always think *first* about "who" and *then* about what.

STAGE 2: DISCIPLINED THOUGHT

CONFRONT THE BRUTAL FACTS—THE STOCKDALE PARADOX: Retain unwavering faith that you can and will prevail in the end, regardless of the difficulties, *and at the same time* have the discipline to confront the most brutal facts of your current reality, whatever they might be.

THE HEDGEHOG CONCEPT: Greatness comes about by a series of good decisions consistent with a simple, coherent concept—a "hedgehog concept." The hedgehog concept is an operating model that reflects understanding of three intersecting circles: what you can be the best in the world at, what you are deeply passionate about, and what best drives your economic or resource engine.

STAGE 3: DISCIPLINED ACTION

CULTURE OF DISCIPLINE: Disciplined people who engage in disciplined thought and who take disciplined action—operating with freedom within a framework of responsibilities: this is the cornerstone of a culture that creates greatness. People do not have jobs; they have *responsibilities*.

THE FLYWHEEL: There is no single defining action, no grand program, no one killer innovation, no solitary lucky break, no miracle moment. Rather, the process resembles relentlessly pushing a giant heavy flywheel, turn upon turn, building momentum until a point of breakthrough, and beyond.

STAGE 4: BUILDING GREATNESS TO LAST

CLOCK BUILDING, NOT TIME TELLING: Truly great organizations prosper through multiple generations of leaders, the exact opposite of being built around a single great leader, great idea, or specific program. Leaders in great organizations build catalytic mechanisms to stimulate progress and do not depend upon having a charismatic personality to get things done; indeed, many have had a "charisma bypass."

PRESERVE THE CORE/STIMULATE PROGRESS: Enduring great organizations are characterized by a fundamental duality. On the one hand, they have a set of timeless core values and core reason for being that remain constant over long periods of time. On the other hand, they have a relentless drive for change and progress—a creative compulsion that often manifests in BHAGs (Big Hairy Audacious Goals). Great organizations keep clear the difference between their core values (which never change) and operating strategies and cultural practices (which endlessly adapt to a changing world).

NOTES

1. Joseph A. Tainter, *The Collapse of Complex Societies* (New York: Cambridge University Press, 1988), 5, 6, 8–12, 128–152.
2. Andrew Hill and John Wooden, *Be Quick—But Don't Hurry* (New York: Simon & Schuster, 2001), 191.
3. United States Geological Survey, "The Great 1906 San Francisco Earthquake," *Earthquake Hazards Program*, http://earthquake.usgs.gov/regional/nca/1906/18april/index.php; A. W. Clausen, "Bank of America: The Largest Bank Was Once a Plank on the Waterfront," *Nation's Business*, January 1971, 54.
4. Joseph H. Harper, "Observations of the San Francisco Earthquake" *The Virtual Museum of the City of San Francisco* (delivered before the Montana Society of Engineers, January 11, 1908), http://www.sfmuseum.org/1906/harper.html; E. E. Schmitz, "Proclamation by the Mayor," *The Virtual Museum of the City of San Francisco* (on April 18, 1906), http://www.sfmuseum.org/1906.2/killproc.html; Gary Hector, *Breaking the Bank: The Decline of BankAmerica* (Boston: Little, Brown & Company, 1988), 25, 36; A. W. Clausen, "Bank of America: The Largest Bank Was Once a Plank on the Waterfront," *Nation's Business*, January 1971, 54.
5. Gary Hector, *Breaking the Bank: The Decline of BankAmerica* (Boston: Little, Brown & Company, 1988), 32, 50, 62.
6. "A. W. Clausen: Banking on Stability at BankAmerica," *Financial World*, March 15, 1978, 24; "BankAmerica and Citicorp: The New Banking Forces New Strategies," *Business Week*, July 13, 1981, 56.

7. David W. Ewing and Pamela M. Banks, "Listening and Responding to Employees' Concerns: An Interview with A. W. Clausen," *Harvard Business Review,* January/February 1980, 101.

8. G. Christian Hill, "BankAmerica Posts a Record Loss of $640 Million for Second Period," *Wall Street Journal,* July 17, 1986; Richard B. Schmitt, "BankAmerica Denies Rumors on Health As Speculation Briefly Depresses Dollar," *Wall Street Journal,* September 17, 1986; Stock returns source: ©200601 CRSP®, Center for Research in Security Prices. Graduate School of Business, The University of Chicago. Used with permission. All rights reserved. www.crsp.chicagobooth.edu; Richard B. Schmitt, "BankAmerica Denies Rumors on Health As Speculation Briefly Depresses Dollar," *Wall Street Journal,* September 17, 1986; G. Christian Hill, "BankAmerica Cuts Quarterly Payout By 47% in Wake of 2nd-Period Loss," *Wall Street Journal,* August 6, 1985; Jonathan B. Levine, "Clausen May Be the Safe Choice, But Is He the Right One?" *Business Week,* October 27, 1986, 108; Victor F. Zonana, "BankAmerica Considers Sale of Headquarters," *Wall Street Journal,* November 19, 1984; "BankAmerica Completes San Francisco Offices' Sale," *Wall Street Journal,* October 2, 1985; G. David Wallace and Jonathan B. Levine, "BofA Is Becoming The Incredible Shrinking Bank," *Business Week,* January 27, 1986, 78; Gary Hector, *Breaking the Bank: The Decline of BankAmerica* (Boston: Little, Brown & Company, 1988), 219–223; "Founder's Daughter Quits BankAmerica Post," *Wall Street Journal,* March 8, 1985; G. Christian Hill and Richard B. Schmitt, "Salvage Operation: Autocrat Tom Clausen Faces Formidable Task To Save BankAmerica, *Wall Street Journal,* October 17, 1986; Robert M. Bleiberg, "What Price BankAmerica? Better Stewards (Corporate or Otherwise) Went Down on the Titanic," *Barron's,* July 21, 1986, 9.

9. Michael Kolbenschlag, "No Time For A Gentleman," *Forbes,* December 22, 1980, 33.

10. Victor F. Zonana and Kathryn Christensen, "Budging the Giant," *Wall Street Journal,* May 20, 1982; "BankAmerica Plans to Acquire Charles Schwab," *Wall Street Journal,* November 25, 1981; Victor F. Zonana, "The Porches and Saabs at Schwab Aggravate Some at BankAmerica," *Wall Street Journal,* January 20, 1983; "BankAmerica Corp.'s Takeover of Seafirst Took Effect Today," *Wall Street Journal,* July 1, 1983, 2; Victor F. Zonana, "Seafirst Holders Clear BankAmerica Bid For Largest Interstate Banking Takeover," *Wall Street Journal,* June 29, 1983; Gary Hector, "More than Mortgages Ails BankAmerica," *Fortune,* April 1, 1985, 50; "BofA's Brash Fight to Build Deposits," *Business Week,* January 17, 1983, 98.

11. Victor F. Zonana, "Budging the Giant," *Wall Street Journal,* May 20, 1982, 1; Victor F. Zonana, "Stirring Giant: BankAmerica Corp., Seeking a

Turnaround, Seems to Gain Ground," *Wall Street Journal*, January 27, 1984.

12. Victor F. Zonana, "The Porches and Saabs at Schwab Aggravate Some at BankAmerica," *Wall Street Journal*, January 20, 1983.

13. "BofA's Brash Fight to Build Deposits," *Business Week*, January 17, 1983, 98; G. Christian Hill and Mike Tharp, "Stumbling Giant: Big Quarterly Deficit Stuns BankAmerica, Adds Pressure on Chief," *Wall Street Journal*, July 18, 1985; Gary Hector, "More than Mortgages Ails BankAmerica," *Fortune*, April 1, 1985, 50.

14. G. Christian Hill and Mike Tharp, "Stumbling Giant: Big Quarterly Deficit Stuns BankAmerica, Adds Pressure on Chief," *Wall Street Journal*, July 18, 1985.

15. George E. P. Box, J. Stuart Hunter, and William G. Hunter, *Statistics for Experimenters: Design, Innovation, and Discovery, 2nd Edition* (Hoboken: John Wiley, 2005), 440.

16. Jill Bettner, " 'Underpromise, Overperform,' " *Forbes*, January 30, 1984, 88; Robert W. Galvin, *The Idea of Ideas* (Schaumburg, IL: Motorola University Press, 1991), 165.

17. Roger O. Crockett and Peter Elstrom, "How Motorola Lost Its Way," *Business Week*, May 4, 1998, 140.

18. Roger O. Crockett, "A New Company Called Motorola," *Business Week*, April 17, 2000, 86; Rajiv Chandrasekaran, "Motorola's Next Page," *Washington Post*, September 29, 1996; Peter Elstrom, "Motorola Goes for the Hard Cell," *Business Week*, September 23, 1996, 39; "Gartner Dataquest Says Worldwide Mobile Phone Sales in 2001 Declined for First Time in Industry's History," *Gartner Press Release*, March 11, 2002, http://www.gartner.com/5_about/press_releases/2002_03/pr20020311a.jsp; Peter Coy and Ron Stodghill, "Is Motorola a Bit Too Patient?" *Business Week*, February 5, 1996, 150.

19. J. Rufus Fears, *Books That Have Made History: Books That Can Change Your Life* (Chantilly, VA: The Teaching Company Limited Partnership, 2005), audiotapes of lectures by J. Rufus Fears, Part 1, Lecture 2.

20. Motorola, Inc., "Financial Highlights," *2001 Summary Annual Report* (Schaumburg, IL: Motorola, Inc., 2002), 3; Motorola, Inc., "Financial Highlights," *2003 Annual Report* (Schaumburg, IL: Motorola, Inc., 2004), 3.

21. Source: ©200601 CRSP®, Center for Research in Security Prices. Graduate School of Business, The University of Chicago. Used with permission. All rights reserved. www.crsp.chicagobooth.edu.

22. Howard Rudnitsky, "Would You Buy A Used Car From This Man?" *Forbes*, October 23, 1995, 52; Tim W. Ferguson, "Sofa With Your Stereo, Sir?" *Forbes*, July 7, 1997, 46.

23. John R. Wells, "Circuit City Stores, Inc.: Strategic Dilemmas," *Harvard Business School,* case study #9-706-419 (Boston: Harvard Business School Publishing, 2005), 7; Rob Landley, "DIVX Post Mortem," *Motley Fool,* June 21, 1999, http://www.fool.com/portfolios/rulemaker/1999/RuleMaker 990621.htm.

24. "Richard L. Sharp—Circuit City Stores, Inc.—CEO Interview," *The Wall Street Transcript,* November 2, 1998, 1.

25. Peter Spiegel, "Car Crash," *Forbes,* May 17, 1999, 130.

26. De'Ann Weimer, "The Houdini of Consumer Electronics," *Business Week,* June 22, 1998, 88; Dorothy Leonard and Brian DeLacey, "Best Buy Co. Inc. (A): An Innovator's Journey," *Harvard Business School,* case study #9-604-043 (Boston: Harvard Business School Publishing, 2005).

27. John R. Wells and Travis Haglock, "Best Buy Co., Inc.: Competing on the Edge," *Harvard Business School,* case study #9-706-417 (Boston: Harvard Business School Publishing, 2007).

28. Best Buy Co., Inc., *Fiscal 2003 Annual Report* (Richfield, MN: Best Buy Co., Inc., 2003); Best Buy Co., Inc., *Fiscal 2001 Annual Report* (Minneapolis: Best Buy Co., Inc., 2001); John R. Wells and Travis Haglock, "Best Buy Co., Inc.: Competing on the Edge," *Harvard Business School,* case study #9-706-417 (Boston: Harvard Business School Publishing, 2007); Balaji Chakravarthy and V. Kasturi Rangan, "Best Buy," *Harvard Business School,* case study #9-598-016 (Boston: Harvard Business School Publishing, 1997); Best Buy Co., Inc., *1996 Annual Report* (Minneapolis: Best Buy Co., Inc., 1996); Dorothy Leonard and Brian DeLacey, "Best Buy Co. Inc. (A): An Innovator's Journey," *Harvard Business School,* case study #9-604-043 (Boston: Harvard Business School Publishing, 2005); Dale Kurschner, "Best Buy Harder," *CRM,* August 1997, 67; Best Buy Co., Inc., *1999 Annual Report* (Minneapolis: Best Buy Co., Inc., 1999); Best Buy Co., Inc., *2003 Annual Report* (Richfield, MN: Best Buy Co., Inc., 2003); Best Buy Co., Inc., *2006 Annual Report* (Richfield, MN: Best Buy Co., Inc., 2006).

29. Calculation based on 1997 and 2006 revenues of Best Buy and Circuit City, taking half of the increase in revenues Best Buy achieved from 1997 to 2006 and adding that amount to Circuit City's 2006 revenues.

30. Balaji Chakravarthy and V. Kasturi Rangan, "Best Buy," *Harvard Business School,* case study #9-598-016 (Boston: Harvard Business School Publishing, 1997); Source: ©200601 CRSP®, Center for Research in Security Prices. Graduate School of Business, The University of Chicago. Used with permission. All rights reserved. www.crsp.chicagobooth.edu.

31. "Pinching 500 Billion Pennies," *Fortune,* March 1963, 105.

32. William I. Walsh, *The Rise and Decline of the Great Atlantic & Pacific Tea Company* (Secaucus, NJ: Lyle Stuart, Inc., 1986), 78–81.

33. William I. Walsh, *The Rise and Decline of the Great Atlantic & Pacific Tea Company* (Secaucus, NJ: Lyle Stuart, Inc., 1986), 78; Eleanor Johnson Tracy, "How A&P Got Creamed," *Fortune*, January 1973, 103.

34. Peter Z. Grossman, "A&P: Should You Invest Along with the Germans?" *Financial World*, February 15, 1979, 16.

35. Ames Department Stores Inc., "Letter to Shareholders," *1987 Annual Report to Stockholders* (Rocky Hill, CT: Ames Department Stores, Inc., 1988).

36. Elizabeth Rourke (updated by David E. Salamie), "Ames Department Stores, Inc." *International Directory of Company Histories* 30 (New York: St. James Press, 2000), 54.

37. William Mehlman, "Ames Strikes Discounting Gold in Exurban America," *The Insiders' Chronicle* 6, no. 46 (November 16, 1981): 1; Peter Hisey, "Herb Gilman: 'The Concept Is So Simple'," *Discount Store News* 27, no. 11 (May 23, 1988): 49; "Ames: Small-Town Discount Giant Trading Up, Not Away From Roots," *Chain Store Age,* February 1982, 25; Jeff Malester, "Ames Aims at Growth by Changing Image," *Retailing Home Furnishings* 57 (August 22, 1983): 6; Al Heller, "Gilman's Informality Spurs Creativity, Growth at Ames," *Discount Store News* 24 (August 19, 1985): 1.

38. Source: ©200601 CRSP®, Center for Research in Security Prices. Graduate School of Business, The University of Chicago. Used with permission. All rights reserved. www.crsp.chicagobooth.edu.

39. Elizabeth Rourke (updated by David E. Salamie), "Ames Department Stores, Inc.," *International Directory of Company Histories* 30 (New York: St. James Press, 2000), 54; Wal-Mart Stores, Inc., "History Timeline," *Wal-Mart: History*, http://walmartstores.com/AboutUs/297.aspx.

40. Source: ©200601 CRSP®, Center for Research in Security Prices. Graduate School of Business, The University of Chicago. Used with permission. All rights reserved. www.crsp.chicagobooth.edu.

41. Personal conversation with author.

42. Steven Jacober, "Ames Redefines Itself at $2 Billion," *Discount Merchandiser*, August 1988, 22; Peter Hisey, "Herb Gilman: 'The Concept Is So Simple,'" *Discount Store News* 27, no. 11 (May 23, 1988): 49.

43. Ames Department Stores, Inc., "Letter to Shareholders," *1988 Annual Report to Stockholders* (Rocky Hill, CT: Ames Department Stores, Inc., 1989); Eric N. Berg, "Ames's Rocky Retailing Marriage," *New York Times*, April 11, 1990.

44. Source: ©200601 CRSP®, Center for Research in Security Prices. Graduate School of Business, The University of Chicago. Used with permission. All rights reserved. www.crsp.chicagobooth.edu.

45. Mike Duff, "Discount Veteran Ames to Liquidate After 44 Years," *DSN Retailing Today* 41, no. 16 (August 26, 2002): 1.

46. Ames Department Stores, Inc., "Letter to Shareholders," *1988 Annual Report to Stockholders* (Rocky Hill, CT: Ames Department Stores, Inc., 1989); Joseph Pereira, "Digesting Zayre Gives Ames Heartburn," *Wall Street Journal,* December 28, 1989; Eric N. Berg, "Ames's Rocky Retailing Marriage," *New York Times,* April 11, 1990; Pete Hisey, "What Went Wrong at Ames?" *Discount Store News* 29, no. 9 (May 7, 1990): 1.

47. Motorola, Inc., *1995 Summary Annual Report* (Schaumburg, IL: Motorola, Inc., 1996).

48. John Simons, "Will R&D Make Merck Hot Again?" *Fortune,* July 8, 2002, 89.

49. "HP Files 5,000 Patent Applications Worldwide in 2001," *HP Press Release* (Palo Alto: Hewlett-Packard Company), February 6, 2002.

50. Alan Farnham, "America's Most Admired Company," *Fortune,* February 7, 1994, 50; Marshall Loeb, "How To Grow A New Product Every Day," *Fortune,* November 14, 1994, 269.

51. "Where Do They Get All Those Ideas?" *Machine Design,* January 26, 1995, 40; Lornet Turnbull, "Ohio-Based Rubbermaid Inc. Heeds Findings from Consumer Focus Groups," *Akron Beacon Journal,* February 18, 1996.

52. Wolfgang R. Schmitt, "A Growth Strategy," *Executive Excellence,* August 1994, 17; Tricia Welsh, "Best and Worst Corporate Reputations," *Fortune,* February 7, 1994, 58; Alan Farnham, "America's Most Admired Company," *Fortune,* February 7, 1994, 50; Marshall Loeb, "How To Grow A New Product Every Day," *Fortune,* November 14, 1994, 269; Lornet Turnbull, "Ohio-Based Rubbermaid Inc. Heeds Findings from Consumer Focus Groups," *Akron Beacon Journal,* February 18, 1996.

53. Lee Smith, "Rubbermaid Goes Thump," *Fortune,* October 2, 1995, 90; Geoffrey Colvin, "From the Most Admired to Just Acquired: How Rubbermaid Managed to Fail," *Fortune,* November 23, 1998, 32.

54. Glen Gamboa, "Rubbermaid Corp. Is Proposing a Nice, Neat Solution," *Akron Beacon Journal,* October 22, 1998; Glen Gamboa, "Rubbermaid Seeks Boost Through 'Solutions' Marketing," *Akron Beacon Journal,* July 28, 1997; Raju Narisetti, "Rubbermaid's Plan to Buy Graco Is Eclipsed by Poor Profit Forecast," *Wall Street Journal,* September 5, 1996; "Rubbermaid Completes Acquisition," *Discount Store News* 35, no. 21 (November 4, 1996): 43; Claudia H. Deutsch, "A Giant Awakens, To Yawns: Is Rubbermaid Reacting Too Late?" *New York Times,* December 22, 1996; Matt Murray, "Rubbermaid Tries to Regain Lost Stature," *Wall Street Journal,* December 6, 1995; Susan Sowa, "Restructuring May Salvage Rubbermaid," *Rubber & Plastics News* 25, no. 10 (December 18, 1995): 7; Lornet Turnbull, "Ohio-Based Rubbermaid Inc. Heeds Findings from Consumer Focus Groups," *Akron Beacon Journal,* February 18, 1996.

55. Geoffrey Colvin, "From the Most Admired to Just Acquired: How Rubbermaid Managed to Fail," *Fortune*, November 23, 1998, 32; Glenn Gamboa, "Rubbermaid Corp. Is Proposing a Nice, Neat Solution," *Akron Beacon Journal*, August 6, 1997; "Buy Merges Rubbermaid's Products, Newell's Management," *Akron Beacon Journal*, October 22, 1998; Claudia H. Deutsch, "Newell Buying Rubbermaid in $5.8 Billion Deal," *New York Times*, October 22, 1998.

56. Amy Barrett and Larry Armstrong, "Merck Takes Some Growth Pills," *Business Week*, October 12, 1998, 78; Gardiner Harris, "Cold Turkey: How Merck Intends to Ride Out a Wave of Patent Expirations," *Wall Street Journal*, February 9, 2000.

57. Clark Gilbert and Ratna G. Sarkar, "Merck: Conflict and Change," *Harvard Business School*, case study #9-805-079 (Boston: Harvard Business School Publishing, 2005).

58. Amy Barrett and Larry Armstrong, "Merck Takes Some Growth Pills," *Business Week*, October 12, 1998, 78.

59. Merck & Co., Inc., *Merck 1998 Annual Report* (Whitehouse Station, NJ: Merck & Co., Inc., 1999), 3.

60. Merck & Co., Inc., *Merck 1999 Annual Report* (Whitehouse Station, NJ: Merck & Co., Inc., 2000); John Simons and David Stipp, "Will Merck Survive Vioxx?" *Fortune*, November 1, 2004, 90.

61. Eduardo Ortiz, "Market Withdrawal of Vioxx: Is It Time to Rethink the Use of COX-2 Inhibitors?" *Journal of Managed Care Pharmacy* 10, no. 6 (November/December 2004): 551–554; Claire Bombardier, Loren Laine, Alise Reicin, et al. for the VIGOR Study Group, "Comparison of Upper Gastrointestinal Toxicity of Rofecoxib and Naproxen in Patients With Rheumatoid Arthritis," *New England Journal of Medicine* 343, no. 21 (November 23, 2000): 1520–1528, http://content.nejm.org/cgi/content/full/343/21/1520.

62. Peter S. Kim and Alise S. Reicin, "Refecoxib, Merck and the FDA," *New England Journal of Medicine* 351, no. 27 (December 30, 2004): 2875–2878; John Simons and David Stipp, "Will Merck Survive Vioxx?" *Fortune*, November 1, 2004, 90.

63. Merck & Co., Inc., *Annual Report 2002* (Whitehouse Station, NJ: Merck & Co., Inc., 2003); Merck & Co., Inc., *Annual Report 2004* (Whitehouse Station, NJ: Merck & Co., Inc., 2005); Susan Dentzer, "Drug Failure," *Online NewsHour*, November 18, 2004, http://www.pbs.org/newshour/bb/health/july-dec04/vioxx_11–18.html.

64. Eric J. Topol, "Failing the Public Health—Rofecoxib, Merck, and the FDA," *New England Journal of Medicine* 351, no. 17 (October 21, 2004): 1701–1709; Debabrata Mukherjee, Steven E. Nissen, and Eric J. Topol, "Risk of Cardiovascular Events Associated with Selective COX-2 Inhibitors," *Journal of the*

American Medical Association 286, no. 8 (August 22, 2001): 954–959; Daniel H. Solomon, Sebastian Schneeweiss, Robert J. Glynn, et al., "Relationship Between Selective Cyclooxygenase-2 Inhibitors and Acute Myocardial Infarction in Older Adults," *Circulation* 109 (April 19, 2004): 2068–2073, http://circ.ahajournals.org/cgi/content/full/109/17/2068.

65. Peter S. Kim and Alise S. Reicin, "Rofecoxib, Merck and the FDA," *New England Journal of Medicine* 351, no. 27 (December 30, 2004): 2875–2878.

66. Merck & Co., Inc., *Annual Report 2004* (Whitehouse Station, NJ: Merck & Co., Inc., 2005), 21.

67. Brooke A. Masters and Marc Kaufman, "Painful Withdrawal for Makers of Vioxx," *Washington Post*, October 18, 2004.

68. Christopher Rowland, "CEO Defends Merck on Vioxx: Confirmation of Woes Came 'Out of Blue,'" *Boston Globe*, October 9, 2004, http://www.boston.com/business/articles/2004/10/09/ceo_defends_merck_on_vioxx; Merck & Co., Inc. "Company Statements," *VIOXX® (rofecoxib) Information Center*, http://www.merck.com/newsroom/vioxx/archive.html#company_statements.

69. John Simons and David Stipp, "Will Merck Survive Vioxx?" *Fortune*, November 1, 2004, 90.

70. George W. Merck, "Talk by George W. Merck at the Medical College of Virginia at Richmond," December 1, 1950.

71. Jim Collins, *Good to Great: Why Some Companies Make the Leap . . . And Others Don't* (New York: HarperCollins, 2001).

72. G. Christian Hill and Mike Tharp, "Stumbling Giant," *Wall Street Journal*, July 18, 1985.

73. Garrett G. Fagan, *Emperors of Rome* (Chantilly, VA: The Teaching Company Limited Partnership, 2007), audiotapes of lectures by Garrett G. Fagan, Lectures 3–6, 10.

74. Ed Viesturs and David Roberts, *No Shortcuts to the Top* (New York: The Doubleday Broadway Publishing Group, 2006), 158.

75. Jill Bettner, "'Underpromise, Overperform,'" *Forbes*, January 30, 1984, 88; Motorola, Inc., "Note 2 to Consolidated Financial Statements," *1996 Summary Annual Report* (Schaumburg, IL: Motorola, Inc., 1997).

76. Sydney Finkelstein and Shade H. Sanford, "Learning from Corporate Mistakes: The Rise and Fall of Iridium," *Organizational Dynamics* 29, no. 2 (November 2000): 138–148.

77. Sydney Finkelstein and Shade H. Sanford, "Learning from Corporate Mistakes: The Rise and Fall of Iridium," *Organizational Dynamics* 29, no. 2 (November 2000): 138–148.

78. Rajiv Chandrasekaran, "Motorola's Next Page: The Cellular Giant and

Onetime Stock Star Seeks Ways to Renew Its Growth," *Washington Post*, September 29, 1996.

79. Motorola, Inc., "Letter to Stockholders," *1997 Summary Annual Report* (Schaumburg, IL: Motorola, Inc., 1998), 6.

80. Sydney Finkelstein and Shade H. Sanford, "Learning from Corporate Mistakes: The Rise and Fall of Iridium," *Organizational Dynamics* 29, no. 2 (November 2000): 138–148.

81. Motorola, Inc., *1999 Proxy Statement* (Schaumburg, IL: Motorola, Inc., 2000), http://media.corporate-ir.net/media_files/irol/90/90829/proxies/mot_000324_1999_proxy.htm.

82. Caleb Pirtle III, *Engineering the World: Stories from the First 75 Years of Texas Instruments* (Dallas: Southern Methodist University Press, 2005), 153; Joan Terrall, "Texas Instruments, Incorporated: 1983," *Harvard Business School,* case study #9-184-109 (Boston: Harvard Business School Publishing, 1984), 10.

83. Robert Ristelhueber, "Texas Tornado," *Electronic Business* 23, no. 12 (December 1997): 35.

84. Svetlana Josifovska, "Deep in the Heart of Texas Instruments," *Electronic Business* 26, no. 10 (October 2000): 116; Peter Burrows and Jonathan B. Levine, "TI is Moving Up in the World," *Business Week*, August 2, 1993, 46; Jim Bartimo, "TI Bets Most of Its Marbles On Chips," *Business Week*, January 29, 1990, 73; Kyle Pope, "Texas Instruments Places Hopes On Chip," *Wall Street Journal*, March 10, 1994; Robert Ristelhueber, "Texas Tornado," *Electronic Business* 23, no. 12 (December 1997): 35; Caleb Pirtle III, *Engineering the World: Stories from the First 75 Years of Texas Instruments* (Dallas: Southern Methodist University Press, 2005), 169–171.

85. Edward R. Tufte, *Visual Explanations: Images and Quantities, Evidence and Narrative* (Cheshire, CT: Graphics Press, 1997), 38–53; Diane Vaughan, *The Challenger Launch Decision: Risky Technology, Culture, and Deviance at NASA* (Chicago: University of Chicago Press, 1996), 278–433.

86. W. L. Gore, conversation with author during an executive session.

87. American Alpine Club, Inc., *Accidents in North American Mountaineering, 1989* (New York: The American Alpine Club, Inc., 1989): rescue ranger at the scene of the accident, conversation with author.

88. Louis V. Gerstner, Jr., *Who Says Elephants Can't Dance? Inside IBM's Historic Turnaround* (New York: HarperCollins, 2002), 204.

89. "Every Dog Needs His Flea," *Forbes*, May 15, 1975, 131.

90. "Scott Paper: Back On Its Feet," *Forbes*, December 15, 1976, 69.

91. "No-Longer-So-Great Scott," *Forbes*, August 1, 1972, 25.

92. "Scott Paper: Back On Its Feet," *Forbes*, December 15, 1976, 69.

93. Stuart C. Gilson and Jeremy Cott, "Scott Paper Company," *Harvard Business School,* case study #9-296-048 (Boston: Harvard Business School Publishing, 1997); Albert J. Dunlap and Bob Andelman, *Mean Business: How I Save Bad Companies and Make Good Companies Great* (New York: Fireside, 1997), 11.

94. "Now An Outsider Will Run Scott Paper," *Business Week,* April 23, 1979, 39; Jean A. Briggs, "Too Little, Too Late?" *Forbes,* July 5, 1982, 88; "Scott Paper Fights Back, At Last," *Business Week,* February 16, 1981, 104.

95. Tom Schmitz, "How Platt Got to the Top of HP," *San Jose Mercury News,* July 18, 1992; Peter Burrows, "Twists in HP's CEO Search," *Business Week,* June 14, 1999, 49; "HP Names Carly Fiorina President and CEO," *Business Wire,* July 19, 1999; Christopher Springmann, "The Best Job in the World," *Across the Board,* May/June, 2003; "Veterans of Value," *Chief Executive,* September 2002.

96. Michael Beer, Rakesh Khurana, and James Weber, "Hewlett-Packard: Culture in Changing Times," *Harvard Business School,* case study #9-404-087 (Boston: Harvard Business School Publishing, 2005), 15; Gregory C. Rogers, "Human Resources at Hewlett-Packard (A)," *Harvard Business School,* case study #9-495-051 (Boston: Harvard Business School Publishing, 1995), 25; Dean Takahashi, "Profits Rise 41%, But H-P Is Unhappy With Growth," *San Jose Mercury News,* May 18, 1995; Peter Burrows, *Backfire: Carly Fiorina's High-Stakes Battle for the Soul of Hewlett-Packard* (Hoboken, NJ: John Wiley & Sons, 2003), 83.

97. Peter Burrows, *Backfire: Carly Fiorina's High-Stakes Battle for the Soul of Hewlett-Packard* (Hoboken, NJ: John Wiley & Sons, 2003), 83; George Anders, *Perfect Enough: Carly Fiorina and the Reinvention of Hewlett-Packard* (New York: Penguin Group, 2003); Hewlett-Packard Company, *1993 Form 10-K* (Palo Alto, CA: Hewlett-Packard Company, 1994).

98. Tom Schmitz, "How Platt Got to the Top of HP," *San Jose Mercury News,* July 18, 1992; Quentin Hardy, "All Carly All the Time," *Forbes,* December 13, 1999, 138.

99. Julie Creswell and Dina Bass, "Ranking the 50 Most Powerful Women: *Fortune*'s First Annual Look at the Women Who Most Influence Corporate America," *Fortune,* October 12, 1998.

100. Carly Fiorina, *Tough Choices: A Memoir* (New York: Penguin Group, 2006), 171–172.

101. George Anders, *Perfect Enough: Carly Fiorina and the Reinvention of Hewlett-Packard* (New York: Penguin Group, 2003), 63; Peter Burrows and Peter Elstrom, "The Boss," *Business Week,* August 2, 1999, 76; Peter Burrows, *Backfire: Carly Fiorina's High-Stakes Battle for the Soul of Hewlett-Packard* (Hoboken, NJ: John Wiley & Sons, 2003), 136–137.

102. Louis V. Gerstner, Jr., *Who Says Elephants Can't Dance? Inside IBM's Historic Turnaround* (New York: HarperCollins, 2002), 54.

103. Louis V. Gerstner, Jr., *Who Says Elephants Can't Dance? Inside IBM's Historic Turnaround* (New York: HarperCollins, 2002), 30.

104. George Anders, "The Carly Chronicles," *Fast Company*, February 2003; Peter Burrows, *Backfire: Carly Fiorina's High-Stakes Battle for the Soul of Hewlett-Packard* (Hoboken, NJ: John Wiley & Sons, 2003), 148; David Packard, *The HP Way: How Bill Hewlett and I Built Our Company* (New York: HarperCollins, 2005).

105. George Anders, *Perfect Enough: Carly Fiorina and the Reinvention of Hewlett-Packard* (New York: Penguin Group, 2003), 64–79; Peter Burrows, *Backfire: Carly Fiorina's High-Stakes Battle for the Soul of Hewlett-Packard* (Hoboken, NJ: John Wiley & Sons, 2003), 135–156; Carly Fiorina, *Tough Choices: A Memoir* (New York: Penguin Group, 2006), 195.

106. Quentin Hardy, "All Carly All the Time," *Forbes*, December 13, 1999, 138.

107. Tom Quinlan, "Transition at the Top for HP: Platt Bows Out as CEO, Ushering in Fiorina," *San Jose Mercury News*, August 18, 1999; Peter Burrows and Peter Elstrom, "The Boss," *Business Week*, August 2, 1999, 76.

108. Louis V. Gerstner, Jr., *Who Says Elephants Can't Dance? Inside IBM's Historic Turnaround* (New York: HarperCollins, 2002), 36, 68.

109. Louis V. Gerstner, Jr., *Who Says Elephants Can't Dance? Inside IBM's Historic Turnaround* (New York: HarperCollins, 2002), 223.

110. David Kirkpatrick, "Lou Gerstner's First 30 Days," *Fortune*, May 31, 1993, 57; Louis V. Gerstner, Jr., *Who Says Elephants Can't Dance? Inside IBM's Historic Turnaround* (New York: HarperCollins, 2002), 56–57.

111. Peter Burrows, *Backfire: Carly Fiorina's High-Stakes Battle for the Soul of Hewlett-Packard* (Hoboken, NJ: John Wiley & Sons, 2003), 76.

112. Carly Fiorina, *Tough Choices: A Memoir* (New York: Penguin Group, 2006), 180.

113. Carly Fiorina, *Tough Choices: A Memoir* (New York: Penguin Group, 2006), 292–294, 303.

114. "HP Sends Letter to Shareowners on Value of Compaq Merger," *Business Wire*, January 18, 2002.

115. Pallavi Gogoi, "Circuit City: Due for a Change?" *BusinessWeek.com*, February 29, 2008, http://www.businessweek.com/bwdaily/dnflash/content/feb2008/d b20080229_251654.htm; Pallavi Gogoi, "Is Circuit City Up for Sale?" *BusinessWeek.com*, April 8, 2008, http://www.businessweek.com/bwdaily/dnflash/content/apr2008/db2008048_602083.htm; Pallavi Gogoi, "Circuit City's Secret Service Plan," *BusinessWeek.com*, August 24, 2008, http://www.businessweek.com/investor/content/aug2006/pi2006 0824_857413.htm; Circuit City Stores, Inc., *Annual Report 2006* (Richmond,

VA: Circuit City Stores, Inc., 2006); Circuit City Stores, Inc., *Annual Report 2007* (Richmond, VA: Circuit City Stores, Inc., 2007); Circuit City Stores, Inc., *Annual Report 2008* (Richmond, VA: Circuit City Stores, Inc., 2008); Louis Llovio, "No Deal for Circuit City," *Times-Dispatch*, July 2, 2008.

116. "Scott Paper Fights Back, At Last," *Business Week*, February 16, 1981, 104; Bill Saporito, "Scott Isn't Lumbering Anymore," *Fortune*, September 30, 1985, 48.

117. Ames Department Stores, Inc., *Annual Reports*, for years 1992–2000 (Rocky Hill, CT: Ames Department Stores, Inc., 1993–2001); Pete Hisey, "Ames Nears Day of Reckoning," *Discount Store News*, August 6, 1990, 1; Jeffrey Arlen, "Fashioning the Turn Around at Ames," *Discount Store News*, April 18, 1994, A10; Don Kaplan, "Ames Redefines Its Niche in the Northeast," *Daily News Record*, October 14, 1994, 3; Dianne M. Pogoda, "Ames is Battling Back," *WWD*, October 26, 1994, 10; Donna Boyle Schwartz, "Hanging Tough," *HFN—The Weekly Newspaper for the Home Furnishing Network*, November 20, 1995, 1; James Mammarella, "Joe Ettore: President, CEO, Ames," *Discount Store News*, December 4, 1995, 36; Valerie Seckler, "Ames's Strategy for Survival," *WWD*, March 19, 1997, 20; Joyce R. Ochs, "Anatomy of a Bankruptcy," *Business Credit 99*, no. 9 (October 1997): 20; Jean E. Palmieri, "At the Magic Show, Ames' Buyers Will Be Seeking the Next Wave in Tops," *Daily News Record*, February 22, 1999, 18; Mike Duff, "Discount Veteran Ames to Liquidate After 44 Years," *DSN Retailing Today*, August 26, 2002, 1.

118. "A&P's Ploy: Cutting Prices to Turn a Profit," *Business Week*, May 20, 1972, 76; William I. Walsh, *The Rise and Decline of the Great Atlantic & Pacific Tea Company* (Secaucus, NJ: Lyle Stuart, Inc., 1986), 146; Mary Bralove, "Price War in Supermarkets Imperils Some As A&P Sets Out to Regain Market Share," *Wall Street Journal*, July 21, 1972; "A&P's 'Price War' Bites Broadly and Deeply," *Business Week*, September 30, 1972, 56; Eleanor Johnson Tracy, "How A&P Got Creamed," *Fortune*, January 1973, 103; Mary Bralove, "A&P Goes Outside Ranks for First Time, Picks Scott to Assume Eventual Command," *Wall Street Journal*, December 11, 1974; Mary Bralove, "New A&P Chairman Unveils 5-Year Plan to Reverse Chain's Declining Fortunes," *Wall Street Journal*, February 7, 1975; "National Tea's Loss is A&P's Gain," *Business Week*, October 18, 1976, 39; "A&P Puts Big Money On its Family Marts," *Business Week*, January 23, 1978, 50; Peter W. Bernstein, "Jonathan Scott's Surprising Failure at A&P," *Fortune*, November 6, 1978, 34; Peter Z. Grossman, "A&P: Should You Invest Along With the Germans?" *Financial World*, February 15, 1979, 16; Gay Sands Miller, "A&P's New President Isn't Signaling Any Retrenchment Wave Despite Deficit," *Wall Street Journal*, May 2, 1980.

119. Roger O. Crockett, "A New Company Called Motorola," *Business Week*, April 17, 2000, 86.

120. Motorola, Inc., *1999 Summary Annual Report* (Schaumburg, IL: Motorola, Inc., 2000).

121. Source: ©200601 CRSP®, Center for Research in Security Prices. Graduate School of Business, The University of Chicago. Used with permission. All rights reserved. www.crsp.chicagobooth.edu.

122. Motorola, Inc., *2000 Summary Annual Report* (Schaumburg, IL: Motorola, Inc., 2001).

123. Barnaby Feder, "Motorola Picks an Outsider to Be Its Chief Executive," *New York Times*, December 17, 2003; Barnaby J. Feder, "New Chief to Take Reins as Motorola Takes on Challenge of Rivals," *New York Times*, January 3, 2004; Laurie J. Flynn, "Motorola Replaces Chief With an Insider," *New York Times*, December 1, 2007.

124. Texas Instruments Inc., "Interactive Timeline," *History of Innovation* (Dallas: Texas Instruments, Inc., 2008), http://www.ti.com/corp/docs/company/history/interactivetimeline.shtml; Erick Schonfeld, "Stetsons Off to Texan Technology," *Fortune*, April 17, 1995, 20; Brian O'Reilly, "Texas Instruments: New Boss, Big Job," *Fortune*, July 8, 1985, 60; "Texas Instruments Inc.," *Business and Company Resource Center* (Farmington Hills, MI: The Gale Group, Inc., 2006), document number: 12501307109; Steve Lohr, "Jerry R. Junkins, 58, Dies; Headed Texas Instruments," *New York Times*, May 30, 1996.

125. Caleb Pirtle III, *Engineering the World: Stories from the First 75 Years of Texas Instruments* (Dallas: Southern Methodist University Press, 2005), 144–146; Peter Burrows and Jonathan B. Levine, "TI is Moving Up in the World," *Business Week*, August 2, 1993, 46.

126. Karen Blumenthal, "Texas Instruments Focuses on Youth as it Names Engibous President, CEO," *Wall Street Journal*, June 21, 1996; Robert Ristelhueber, "Texas Tornado," *Electronic Business* 23, no. 12 (December 1997): 35; Erick Schonfeld, "Hotter than Intel," *Fortune*, October 11, 1999, 179; Elisa Williams, "Mixed Signals," *Forbes*, May 28, 2001, 80.

127. Andrew Park, "For Every Gizmo, a TI Chip," *Business Week*, August 16, 2004, 52.

128. Source: ©200601 CRSP®, Center for Research in Security Prices. Graduate School of Business, The University of Chicago. Used with permission. All rights reserved. www.crsp.chicagobooth.edu.

129. "Office Equipment," *Forbes*, January 1, 1963, 61.

130. "Addressograph Multigraph Had a Great Fall," *Forbes*, September 15, 1973, 88; "Taking On Xerox With a Fast Copier," *Business Week*, April 26, 1969, 78; "The Man on the Spot," *Forbes*, June 1, 1975, 24; David Pauly and James

C. Jones, "Corporations: Roy Ash's Challenge," *Newsweek*, December 13, 1976, 90; "Addressograph Gets the Roy Ash Treatment," *Business Week*, March 21, 1977, 36.

131. David Pauly and James C. Jones, "Corporations: Roy Ash's Challenge," *Newsweek*, December 13, 1976, 90; "AM International: When Technology Was Not Enough," *Business Week*, January 25, 1982, 62.

132. "Addressograph Jumps Into Word Processing," *Business Week*, July 4, 1977, 19; Louis Kraar, "Roy Ash is Having Fun at Addressogrief-Multigrief," *Fortune*, February 27, 1978, 46; "AM International: When Technology Was Not Enough," *Business Week*, January 25, 1982, 62; Andrew Baxter, "AM International Rebuilds on its Old Foundations," *Financial Times*, March 29, 1984; Thomas C. Hayes, "Ash Forced Out of Two AM Posts," *New York Times*, February 24, 1981.

133. Susie Gharib Nazem and Susan Kinsley, "How Roy Ash Got Burned," *Fortune*, April 6, 1981, 71.

134. "AM International: When Technology Was Not Enough," *Business Week*, January 25, 1982, 62.

135. "Addressograph Multigraph Had a Great Fall," *Forbes*, September 15, 1973, 88; "How AM is Pulling Itself Up Again," *Business Week*, June 13, 1983, 37; Andrew Baxter, "AM International Rebuilds on its Old Foundations," *Financial Times*, March 29, 1984; "AM International: Profits Are In, High Tech's Out," *Business Week*, July 7, 1986, 77.

136. "Addressograph Gets Ash and $2.7 Million," *Business Week*, October 4, 1976, 31; "Up From the Ashes," *Forbes*, April 16, 1979, 104; Leslie Wayne, "AM International's Struggle," *New York Times*, June 20, 1981; "AM Files Chapter 11 Petition," *New York Times*, April 15, 1982; "Cleaning Up the Mess at AM International," *Business Week*, December 3, 1984, 165; John N. Maclean, "AM Files Again For Chapter 11," *Chicago Tribune*, May 18, 1993.

137. "An Aftershock Stuns AM International," *Business Week*, March 22, 1982, 30.

138. N. R. Kleinfield, "AM's Brightest Years Now Dim Memories," *New York Times*, April 15, 1982.

139. Stuart C. Gilson and Jeremy Cott, "Scott Paper Company," *Harvard Business School*, case study #9-296-048 (Boston: Harvard Business School Publishing, 1997); Albert J. Dunlap and Bob Andelman, *Mean Business: How I Save Bad Companies and Make Good Companies Great* (New York: Fireside, 1997), 11.

140. John A. Byrne and Joseph Weber, "The Shredder: Did CEO Dunlap Save Scott Paper—or Just Pretty It Up?" *Business Week*, January 15, 1996, 56.

141. John A. Byrne, *Chainsaw: The Notorious Career of Al Dunlap in the Era of Profit-at-Any-Price* (New York: HarperCollins Publishers, 2003).

142. John A. Byrne and Joseph Weber, "The Shredder: Did CEO Dunlap Save Scott Paper—or Just Pretty It Up?" *Business Week,* January 15, 1996, 56; Albert J. Dunlap and Bob Andelman, *Mean Business: How I Save Bad Companies and Make Good Companies Great* (New York: Fireside, 1997), 21.

143. "Commander McDonald of Zenith," *Fortune,* June 1945, 141.

144. Richard Hammer, "Zenith Bucks the Trend," *Fortune,* December 1960, 128; "Troubled Zenith Battles Stiffer Competition," *Business Week,* October 10, 1977, 128.

145. Richard Hammer, "Zenith Bucks the Trend," *Fortune,* December 1960, 128; "Sam Kaplan 'That's Our Plan,'" *Forbes,* May 15, 1968, 80; "Zenith Fills the Rooms at the Top," *Business Week,* May 16, 1970, 62; "The Big Winner," *Forbes,* April 1, 1974; "Every Dog Needs His Flea," *Forbes,* May 15, 1975, 131; "Troubled Zenith Battles Stiffer Competition," *Business Week,* October 10, 1977, 128; Bob Tamarkin, "Zenith's New Hope," *Forbes,* March 31, 1980, 32.

146. "Zenith to Jimmy Carter: Help!" *Forbes,* December 15, 1976, 43; "Troubled Zenith Battles Stiffer Competition," *Business Week,* October 10, 1977, 128.

147. Bob Tamarkin, "Zenith's New Hope," *Forbes,* March 31, 1980, 32; "Zenith May Lead the Way in the Video Revolution," *Business Week,* February 23, 1981, 94; "Zenith: The Surprise in Personal Computers," *Business Week,* December 12, 1983, 102; "Zenith Wants to Give the Boob Tube a Brain," *Business Week,* May 6, 1985, 71.

148. "Zenith's Jerry Pearlman Sure is Persistent," *Business Week,* October 2, 1989, 67; "Zenith: The Surprise in Personal Computers," *Business Week,* December 12, 1983, 102.

149. "Zenith is Doing Quite Well, Thank you—In Computers," *Business Week,* July 11, 1988, 80; "Zenith's Jerry Pearlman Sure is Persistent," *Business Week,* October 2, 1989, 67; Lois Therrien, Thane Peterson, and Geoff Lewis, "Why Jerry Pearlman Gave Up His Brainchild," *Business Week,* October 16, 1989, 35; "Zenith's Bright Side and Its Dark Side," *Forbes,* May 2, 1988, 112.

150. Lisa Kartus, "The Strange Folks Picking on Zenith," *Fortune,* December 19, 1988, 79; Lois Therrien, Thane Peterson, and Geoff Lewis, "Why Jerry Pearlman Gave Up His Brainchild," *Business Week,* October 16, 1989, 35; Robert L. Rose, "Zenith Faces Liquidity Crunch in Wake of Price Wars," *Wall Street Journal,* November 11, 1992; "Zenith Dials Up a New CEO," *Business Week,* March 13, 1995; "Getting the Picture," *Crain's Chicago Business* 20, no. 2 (January 13, 1997): 13.

151. Lisa Kartus, "The Strange Folks Picking on Zenith," *Fortune,* December 19, 1988, 79; Lois Therrien, "HDTV Isn't Clearing Up Zenith's Picture," *Business Week,* February 25, 1991, 56; H. Garrett DeYoung, "An Improving

Picture for Zenith?" *Electronic Business*, June 1993, 83; "'A Short Leash' at Zenith," *Business Week*, January 31, 1994, 31; Laxmi Nakarmi, Richard A. Melcher, and Edith Updike, "Will Lucky Goldstar Reach Its Peak with Zenith?" *Business Week*, August 7, 1995, 40; "Zenith Faces Liquidity Crunch in Wake of Price Wars," *Wall Street Journal*, November 11, 1992; Carl Quintanilla and Robert L. Rose, "Zenith Turns to a Turnaround Expert in Its Efforts to Fatten Up Bottom Line," *Wall Street Journal*, January 7, 1998; "Zenith Electronics Corporation: History," *Hoovers*, http://premium .hoovers.com/subscribe/co/history.xhtml?ID=ffffrrjjffffhrtfkfc; Liz Brooks, "Zenith Electronics' New Focus on the Digital Sector Is Discussed," *Adweek Magazine's Technology Marketing* 21, no. 10 (November 2001): 26; "Why Jerry Pearlman Gave Up His Brainchild," *Business Week*, October 16, 1989, 35; "Zenith Wishes on a Lucky-Goldstar," *Business Week*, March 11, 1991; Carol Haber and Chad Fasca, "One Last Rescue for Zenith," *Electronic News* 44, no. 2206 (February 16, 1998): 53.

152. Xerox Corporation, *Annual Report 2002* (Stamford, CT: Xerox Corporation, 2003); Pamela L. Moore, "She's Here to Fix the Xerox," *Business Week*, August 6, 2001, 47; J. P. Donlon, "The X-Factor," *Chief Executive*, June 2008; Anthony Bianco and Pamela L. Moore, "The Downfall: The Inside Story of the Management Fiasco at Xerox," *Business Week*, March 5, 2001, 82.

153. Kevin Maney, "Mulcahy Traces Steps of Xerox's Comeback," *USA Today*, September 21, 2006.

154. Betsy Morris, "The Accidental CEO," *Fortune*, June 23, 2003, 58.

155. Kevin Maney, "Mulcahy Traces Steps of Xerox's Comeback," *USA Today*, September 21, 2006.

156. Kathleen Cholewka, "Xerox's Savior?" *Sales and Marketing Management* 153, no. 4 (April 2001); Patricia Sellers and Cora Daniels, "The 50 Most Powerful Women in American Business," *Fortune*, October 12, 1998, 76; Patricia Sellers, "These Women Rule: Hewlett-Packard's New CEO and President Tops Fortune's Second Annual Ranking of the 50 Most Powerful Women in American Business," *Fortune*, October 25, 1999, 94.

157. Betsy Morris, "The Accidental CEO," *Fortune*, June 23, 2003, 58.

158. Karen Lowry Miller, "The Quiet CEOs," *Newsweek*, December 20, 2004.

159. Jim Collins research team analysis.

160. Nanette Byrnes, "Lessons from a Baptism by Fire," *Business Week*, August 12, 2002, 64.

161. Pamela L. Moore, "She's Here to Fix the Xerox," *Business Week*, August 6, 2001, 47.

162. Betsy Morris, "The Accidental CEO," *Fortune*, June 23, 2003, 58.

163. Nanette Byrnes, "Lessons from a Baptism by Fire," *Business Week*, August 12, 2002, 64; J. P. Donlon, "The X-Factor," *Chief Executive*, June 2008.

164. J. P. Donlon, "The X-Factor," *Chief Executive*, June 2008; Nanette Byrnes, "Lessons from a Baptism by Fire," *Business Week*, August 12, 2002, 64; Pamela L. Moore, "She's Here to Fix the Xerox," *Business Week*, August 6, 2001, 47.

165. J. P. Donlon, "The X-Factor," *Chief Executive*, June 2008.

166. Dick Clark, conversation with author.

167. Joseph A. Schumpeter, *Capitalism, Socialism and Democracy* (New York: Harper Torchbooks, 1962).

168. William Manchester, *The Last Lion: Winston Spencer Churchill, Visions of Glory 1874–1932* (New York: Dell Publishing, 1983), 614, 857, 860, 878–880, 883; J. Rufus Fears, *Churchill* (Chantilly, VA: The Teaching Company Limited Partnership, 2001), audiotapes of lectures by J. Rufus Fears, Lectures 5–12.

169. William Manchester, *The Last Lion: Winston Spencer Churchill, Visions of Glory 1874–1932* (New York: Dell Publishing, 1983), 883; J. Rufus Fears, *Churchill* (Chantilly, VA: The Teaching Company Limited Partnership, 2001), audiotapes of lectures by J. Rufus Fears, Lectures 5–12.

170. William Manchester, *The Last Lion: Winston Spencer Churchill, Visions of Glory 1874–1932* (New York: Dell Publishing, 1983), 32; The Churchill Centre, "We Shall Fight on the Beaches," *Selected Speeches of Winston Churchill,* http://www.winstonchurchill.org/i4a/pages/index.cfm?pageid=393.

171. The Churchill Centre, "Never Give In, Never, Never, Never," *Selected Speeches of Winston Churchill,* http://www.winstonchurchill.org/i4a/pages/index.cfm?pageid=423; J. Rufus Fears, *Churchill* (Chantilly, VA: The Teaching Company Limited Partnership, 2001), audiotapes of lectures by J. Rufus Fears, Lectures 5–12.

172. "How the Rescue Plan Will Work," *Washington Post*, September 8, 2008.

173. Fannie Mae, *Investor Relations: Stock Information,* http://www.fanniemae.com/ir/resources/index.jhtml?s=Stock+Information.

174. Charles Duhigg, "The Reckoning: Pressured to Take More Risk, Fannie Reached Tipping Point," *New York Times*, October 5, 2008.

175. "A Conversation with Vikrim Pandit, CEO of Citigroup," *The Charlie Rose Show*, November 25, 2008, http://www.charlierose.com/view/interview/9653.

176. Timothy L. O'Brien and Jennifer Lee, "A Seismic Shift Under the House of Fannie Mae," *New York Times*, October 3, 2004; Bethany McLean, "The Fall of Fannie Mae," *Fortune*, January 24, 2005, 122; Annys Shin, "Report Details Raines's Clout at Fannie Mae," *Washington Post*, February 24, 2006; James R. Hagerty and Joann S. Lublin, "Mudd Plans Fannie Makeover," *Wall Street Journal*, December 24, 2004; Stephen Labaton and Eric Dash,

"Loan Buyer Accounting Is Faulted," *Washington Post*, February 24, 2006; Terence O'Hara, "The Fannie Mae Report," *Washington Post*, February 24, 2006; Eric Dash and Michael J. de la Merced, "Regulators Denounce Fannie Mae," *New York Times*, May 24, 2006.

177. Fannie Mae, "Letter to Shareholders," *2001 Annual Report* (Washington, DC: Fannie Mae, 2002), 2; Annys Shin,"Examining Fannie Mae; How a Former Chief Helped Shape the Company's Culture," *Washington Post*, May 24, 2006; Russell Roberts, "How Government Stoked the Mania," *Wall Street Journal*, October 3, 2008.

178. Fannie Mae, *2001 Annual Report* (Washington, DC: Fannie Mae, 2002), 9, 49; Janice Revell, "Fannie Mae Is Plenty Safe," *Fortune*, May 27, 2002, 77; Patrick Barta, "Loan Stars: Why Calls Are Rising to Clip Fannie Mae's, Freddie Mac's Wings," *Wall Street Journal*, July 14, 2000.

179. Fannie Mae, "Letter to Shareholders," *2002 Annual Report* (Washington, DC: Fannie Mae, 2003); Fannie Mae, "Letter to Shareholders," *2003 Annual Report* (Washington, DC: Fannie Mae, 2004).

180. Office of Federal Housing Enterprise Oversight, "Report of Findings to Date," *Special Examination of Fannie Mae* (Washington, DC: OFHEO, 2004), i, report released on September 17, 2004.

181. Eric Dash and Stephen Labaton, "The Welcome Mat Is Out," *Washington Post*, February 18, 2006; Fannie Mae, *2005 Form 10-K* (Washington, DC: Fannie Mae, 2006), 52 and 91; Fannie Mae, *2006 Annual Report* (Washington, DC: Fannie Mae, 2007), 37.

182. Annys Shin, "New Paths for Mortgage Giants," *Washington Post*, December 5, 2005.

183. Fannie Mae, "Letter to Shareholders," *2006 Annual Report* (Washington, DC: Fannie Mae, 2007), 5; David S. Hilzenrath, "Fannie, Freddie Face Conflicting Demands," *Washington Post*, December 4, 2007; "End of Illusions; Fannie Mae and Freddie Mac," *Economist*, July 19, 2008; David S. Hilzenrath, "Fannie's Perilous Pursuit of Subprime Loans," *Washington Post*, August 19, 2008.

184. Charles Duhigg, "The Reckoning: Pressured to Take More Risk, Fannie Reached Tipping Point," *New York Times*, October 5, 2008.

185. David S. Hilzenrath, "Fannie Loses $2.2 Billion As Home Prices Fall," *Washington Post,* May 7, 2008; Charles Duhigg, "Mortgage Giants to Buy Fewer Risky Home Loans," *New York Times*, August 9, 2008; "How the Rescue Plan Will Work," *Washington Post*, September 8, 2008.

186. "Office Equipment," *Forbes*, January 1, 1964, 79; "The Competitive Office Equipments," *Financial World*, May 19, 1965, p. 6; "Information Processing," *Forbes*, January 1, 1968, 47.

187. "Taking On Xerox with a Fast Copier," *Business Week*, April 26, 1969, 78;

"Addressograph Multigraph Had a Great Fall," *Forbes*, September 15, 1973, 88; David Pauly and James C. Jones, "Corporations: Roy Ash's Challenge," *Newsweek*, December 13, 1976, 90; "The Man on the Spot," *Forbes*, June 1, 1975, 24.

188. Al Heller, "Gilman's Informality Spurs Creativity, Growth at Ames," *Discount Store News*, August 19, 1985, 1; Elizabeth Rourke and David E. Salamie, "Ames Department Stores, Inc.," *International Directory of Company Histories, Vol. 30* (New York: St. James Press, 2000), 55.

189. Peter Hisey, "Herb Gilman: 'The Concept is So Simple,'" *Discount Store News*, May 23, 1988, 49; Steven Jacober, "Ames Redefines Itself at $2 Billion," *DM*, August 1988, 22; "Building Ames with Careful Shopping," *Discount Store News*, September 25, 1989, 85; Joseph Pereira, "Digesting Zayre Gives Ames Heartburn," *Wall Street Journal*, December 28, 1989; Ames Department Stores, Inc., *1989 Annual Report to Stockholders* (Rocky Hill, CT: Ames Department Stores, Inc., 1990), 13–14.

190. "Under the Wire," *Forbes*, June 15, 1969, 61; Milton Moskowitz, "Bank of America's Rocky Road to Corporate Social Responsibility," *Bankers Magazine*, Autumn 1977, 77. "Why They're Slowing Growth at the World's Biggest Bank," *Business Week*, February 24, 1975, 54.

191. John J. O'Rourke, "Bank of America's Tom Clausen . . . A Man for the Seventies," *Burroughs Clearing House*, January 1970, 1, 21.

192. "The Biggest Bank Bets More on High Risk," *Business Week*, May 22, 1971, 80.

193. "Why They're Slowing Growth at the World's Biggest Bank," *Business Week*, February 24, 1975, 54.

194. "BankAmericard Due to Carry New Name Beginning Next Year," *Wall Street Journal*, August 20, 1976.

195. G. Christian Hill and Mike Tharp, "Stumbling Giant: Big Quarterly Deficit Stuns BankAmerica, Adds Pressure on Chief," *Wall Street Journal*, July 18, 1985; Gary Hector, *Breaking the Bank: The Decline of BankAmerica* (Boston: Little, Brown & Company, 1988), 190–192.

196. Circuit City Stores, Inc., "Management Letter," *Annual Report 1996* (Richmond, VA: Circuit City Stores, Inc, 1996), 4.

197. John R. Wells, "Circuit City Stores, Inc.: Strategic Dilemmas," *Harvard Business School*, case study #9-706-419 (Boston: Harvard Business School Publishing, 2005); Peter Spiegel, "Car Crash," *Forbes*, May 17, 1999.

198. Evan Ramstad, "Circuit City CEO Meets with Rivals to Peddle Alternative DVD Product," *Wall Street Journal*, January 14, 1998; "Richard L. Sharp— Circuit City Stores Inc. (CC)," *Wall Street Transcript*, November 11, 1998.

199. Gregory C. Rogers, "Human Resources at Hewlett-Packard (A)," *Harvard Business School*, case study #9-495-051 (Boston: Harvard Business School

Publishing, 1995); Michael Beer, Rakesh Khurana, and James Weber, "Hewlett-Packard: Culture in Changing Times," *Harvard Business School*, case study #0-404-087 (Boston: Harvard Business School Publishing, 2005).

200. Alan Deutschman, "How H-P Continues to Grow and Grow," *Fortune*, May 2, 1994, 90.

201. Dana Wechsler Linden and Bruce Upbin, "Top Corporate Performance of 1995: 'Boy Scouts on a Rampage,'" *Forbes*, January 1, 1996, 66.

202. John H. Sheridan, "Lew Platt: Creating a Culture for Innovation," *Industry Week*, December 19, 1994, 26; Alan Deutschman, "How H-P Continues to Grow and Grow," *Fortune*, May 2, 1994, 90; Jennifer Telford, "Street-Smart CEO Shapes Hewlett Packard Vision," *Denver Business Journal*, March 1–7, 1996, 1.

203. David Einstein, "Anonymous, Inc.," *Marketing Computers* 15, no. 4 (April 1995): 28; Peter Burrows, "The Printer King Invades Home PCs," *Business Week*, August 21, 1995, 74; Richard A. Shaffer, "The Bittersweet Success of Home PCs," *Forbes*, September 11, 1995, 262; Lee Gomes, "Hewlett-Packard Sets Its PC Bar Higher and Higher," *Wall Street Journal*, September 8, 1997.

204. Arthur M. Louis, "HP to Quit Disk-Drive Business," *San Francisco Chronicle*, July 11, 1996; Tom Quinlan and Scott Thurm, "HP Buys Electronic Card Firm Verifone," *San Jose Mercury News*, April 24, 1997; Nikhil Hutheesing, "HP's Giant ATM," *Forbes*, February 9, 1998, 96.

205. Brian Gillooly, "HP's New Course," *Information Week*, March 20, 1995, 45; Peter Burrows, Geoffrey Smith, and Steven V. Brull, "HP Pictures the Future," *Business Week*, July 7, 1997, 100.

206. Joseph Weber and Rochelle Shoretz, "Is This Rx Too Costly for Merck?" *Business Week*, August 9, 1993, 28; Joseph Weber, "Mr. Nice Guy With a Mission," *Business Week*, November 25, 1996, 132; Merck & Co., Inc., *1995 Annual Report* (Whitehouse Station, NJ: Merck & Co., Inc., 1996).

207. Merck & Co., Inc., "Letter to Shareholders," *Annual Report 2000*, (Whitehouse Station, NJ: Merck & Co., Inc, 2000).

208. John Simons, "Will R&D Make Merck Hot Again?" *Fortune*, July 8, 2002, 89.

209. Merck & Co., Inc., *1998 Annual Report* (Whitehouse Station, NJ: Merck & Co., Inc., 1999), 22.

210. Barnaby J. Feder, "Motorola Will Be Just Fine, Thanks," *New York Times*, October 31, 1993.

211. Karl Schoenberger, "Motorola Bets Big on China," *Fortune*, May 27, 1996, 116.

212. Quentin Hardy, "Unsolid State: Motorola, Broadsided by the Digital Era, Struggles for a Footing," *Wall Street Journal*, April 22, 1998.

213. Karl Schoenberger, "Motorola Bets Big on China," *Fortune,* May 27, 1996, 116; Rick Tetzeli, "And Now for Motorola's Next Trick," *Fortune,* April 28, 1997, 122.

214. Motorola, Inc., *1995 Summary Annual Report* (Schaumburg, IL: Motorola, Inc., 1996), 12.

215. Gary Slutsker, "The Company that Likes to Obsolete Itself," *Forbes,* September 13, 1993, 139; Ronald Henkoff, "Keeping Motorola on a Roll," *Fortune,* April 18, 1994, 67.

216. Lois Therrien, "The Rival Japan Respects," *Business Week,* November 13, 1989, 108; Motorola, Inc., "About Motorola University: The Inventors of Six Sigma," *Motorola University,* http://www.motorola.com/content.jsp?globalObjectId=3079.

217. G. Christian Hill and Ken Yamada, "Staying Power: Motorola Illustrates How An Aged Giant Can Remain Vibrant," *Wall Street Journal,* December 9, 1992.

218. Jim Collins, *Good to Great: How Some Companies Make the Leap . . . and Others Don't* (New York: HarperCollins Publishers, Inc., 2001), 26.

219. Zachary Schiller, "At Rubbermaid, Little Things Mean A Lot," *Business Week,* November 11, 1991, 126.

220. Rahul Jacob, "Thriving in a Lame Economy," *Fortune,* October 5, 1992, 44.

221. Seth Lubove, "Okay, Call Me A Predator," *Forbes,* February 15, 1993, 150.

222. Seth Lubove, "Okay, Call Me A Predator," *Forbes,* February 15, 1993, 150.

223. Wolfgang R. Schmitt, "A Growth Strategy," *Executive Excellence* 11, no. 8 (August 1994): 17.

224. "Scott Paper Fights Back, At Last," *Business Week,* February 16, 1981, 104; "Profits Peak for Scott Paper," *Financial World,* April 22, 1970, 13; Ira U. Cobleigh, "Scott Paper Company," *Commercial and Financial Chronicle,* January 22, 1970, 5; "A Paper Tiger Grows Claws," *Business Week,* August 23, 1969, 100; "Scott Paper: Back On Its Feet," *Forbes,* December 15, 1976, 69.

225. "A Paper Tiger Grows Claws," *Business Week,* August 23, 1969, 100.

226. "Zenith Electronics Corporation," *Electrical & Electronics,* [no date], 123.

227. "Sam Kaplan: 'That's Our Plan,'" *Forbes,* May 15, 1968, 80; "Zenith Electronics Corporation," *Electrical & Electronics,* [no date], 123; "Zenith Fills the Rooms at the Top," *Business Week,* May 16, 1970, 62.

228. "Zenith Fills the Rooms at the Top," *Business Week,* May 16, 1970, 62.

229. "Troubled Zenith Battles Stiffer Competition," *Business Week,* October 10, 1977, 128; "Zenith Radio Corporation (C)," *Harvard Business School,* case study #9-674-095 (Boston: Harvard Business School Publishing, 1977); "Every Dog Needs His Flea," *Forbes,* May 15, 1975, 131.

230. "The Big Winner," *Forbes,* April 1, 1974.

231. Richard Hammer, "Zenith Bucks the Trend," *Fortune*, December 1960, 128; "At Zenith and On the Spot," *Forbes*, September 1, 1961, 19; "Every Dog Needs His Flea," *Forbes*, May 15, 1975, 131.

232. William I. Walsh, *The Rise and Decline of the Great Atlantic & Pacific Tea Company* (Secaucus, NJ: Lyle Stuart, Inc., 1986), 94, 111; "Hermit Kingdom," *Wall Street Journal*, December 12, 1958; "Pinching 500 Billion Pennies," *Fortune*, March 1963, 105; "New Crowd Minds Store for the Tea Company," *Business Week*, June 13, 1964, 90.

233. "Pinching 500 Billion Pennies," *Fortune*, March 1963, 105.

234. William I. Walsh, *The Rise and Decline of the Great Atlantic & Pacific Tea Company* (Secaucus, NJ: Lyle Stuart, Inc., 1986), 94.

235. William I. Walsh, *The Rise and Decline of the Great Atlantic & Pacific Tea Company* (Secaucus, NJ: Lyle Stuart, Inc., 1986), 104–105; Norman C. Miller, Jr., "Ailing A&P," *Wall Street Journal*, April 21, 1964.

236. "A&P's 'Price War' Bites Broadly and Deeply," *Business Week*, September 30, 1972, 56; "Shopping Center Shoot-Out: Price War in Supermarkets Imperils Some as A&P Sets Out to Regain Market Share," *Wall Street Journal*, July 21, 1972.

237. "A&P's Ploy: Cutting Prices to Turn a Profit," *Business Week*, May 20, 1972, 76; William I. Walsh, *The Rise and Decline of the Great Atlantic & Pacific Tea Company* (Secaucus, NJ: Lyle Stuart, Inc., 1986), 146; "A&P's 'Price War' Bites Broadly and Deeply," *Business Week*, September 30, 1972, 56; Eleanor Johnson Tracy, "How A&P Got Creamed," *Fortune*, January 1973, 103; Mary Bralove, "New A&P Chairman Unveils 5-Year Plan to Reverse Chain's Declining Fortunes," *Wall Street Journal*, February 7, 1975; "A&P Puts Big Money On Its Family Marts," *Business Week*, January 23, 1978, 50; "Stumbling Giant," *Wall Street Journal*, January 10, 1978; Peter W. Bernstein, "Jonathan Scott's Surprising Failure at A&P," *Fortune*, November 6, 1978, 34; "German Group Planning to Buy 42% A&P Stake," *Wall Street Journal*, January 17, 1979; Gay Sands Miller, "A&P's New President Isn't Signaling Any Retrenchment Wave Despite Deficit," *Wall Street Journal*, May 2, 1980.

238. "Addressograph Multigraph Had a Great Fall," *Forbes*, September 15, 1973, 88; "Taking on Xerox with a Fast Copier," *Business Week*, April 26, 1969, 78; "The Man on the Spot," *Forbes*, June 1, 1975, 24; David Pauly and James C. Jones, "Corporations: Roy Ash's Challenge," *Newsweek*, December 13, 1976, 90; "AM International: When Technology Was Not Enough," *Business Week*, January 25, 1982, 62; "Addressograph Gets the Roy Ash Treatment," *Business Week*, March 21, 1977, 36; Louis Kraar, "Roy Ash is Having Fun at Addressogrief-Multigrief," *Fortune*, February 27, 1978, 46; Andrew

Baxter, "AM International Rebuilds On Its Old Foundations," *Financial Times*, March 29, 1984; Susie Gharib Nazem, "How Roy Ash Got Burned," *Fortune*, April 6, 1981, 71; "An Aftershock Stuns AM International," *Business Week*, March 22, 1982, 30; N.R. Kleinfield, "AM's Brightest Years Now Dim Memories," *New York Times*, April 15, 1982; "AM Files Chapter 11 Petition," *New York Times*, April 15, 1982.

239. Ames Department Stores, Inc., "Letter to the Shareholders," *Annual Report 1993* (Rocky Hill, CT: Ames Department Stores, Inc., 1993), 2; Ames Department Stores, Inc., "Letter to the Shareholders," *Annual Report 1995* (Rocky Hill, CT: Ames Department Stores, Inc., 1996), 3; Ames Department Stores, Inc., "Letter to Our Shareholders," *Annual Report Fiscal 1999* (Rocky Hill, CT: Ames Department Stores, Inc., 2000), 2; "Ames Nears Day of Reckoning," *Discount Store News*, August 6, 1990, 1; Don Kaplan, "Ames Redefines Its Niche in the Northeast," *Daily News Record*, October 14, 1994, 3; Donna Boyle Schwartz, "Hanging Tough," *HFM: The Weekly Newspaper for Home Furnishing Network*, November 20, 1995, 1; Jean E. Palmieri, "At the Magic Show, Ames' Buyers Will Be Seeking the Next Wave in Tops," *Daily News Record*, February 22, 1999, 18; Mike Duff, "Discount Veteran Ames to Liquidate After 44 yrs," *DSN Retailing Today*, August 26, 2002, 1.

240. Gary Hector, "More Than Mortgages Ails BankAmerica," *Fortune*, April 1, 1985, 50; "Bank of America Rushes Into the Information Age," *Business Week*, April 15, 1985, 110; George Palmer, "Sam Armacost's Sea of Troubles at BankAmerica," *Banker*, September 1985, 18; "BankAmerica: Wrenching Year," *Banker*, March 1986, 7; Richard B. Schmitt and G. Christian Hill, "BankAmerica's Board to Request that Armacost Quit, Sources Say," *Wall Street Journal*, October 10, 1986; Richard B. Schmitt and G. Christian Hill, "BankAmerica Names Clausen Top Executive," *Wall Street Journal*, October 13, 1986; Jonathan B. Levine, "Clausen May Be the Safe Choice, But Is He the Right One?" *Business Week*, October 27, 1986, 108; Richard B. Schmitt, "Reviving Giant," *Wall Street Journal*, July 18, 1988.

241. Circuit City Stores, Inc., *Annual Reports 2002–2007* (Richmond, VA: Circuit City Stores, Inc., 2002–2007); "Circuit City Stores, Inc, (CC)," *Wall Street Journal*, November 5, 1987; Philip H. Dougherty, "Advertising: Research on Haggling Influences Ad Effort," *New York Times*, November 12, 1984; "Circuit City Stores Inc. 9950," *Washington Post*, April 29, 2002; Martha McNeil Hamilton, "Circuit City's New Direction," *Washington Post*, February 16, 2002; Stuart Elliott, "Circuit City Uses an Old Song to Personify Customer Advice," *New York Times*, October 1, 2004; Terence O'Hara, "Circuit City Taps President to be New CEO," *Washington Post*, December 20,

2005; John R. Wells, "Circuit City Stores, Inc.: Strategic Dilemmas," *Harvard Business School,* case study #9-706-419 (Boston: Harvard Business School Publishing, 2005), 7; Pallavi Gogoi, "Circuit City: Due for a Change?" *BusinessWeek.com,* February 29, 2008, http://www.business week.com/bwdaily/dnflash/content/feb2008/db20080229_251654.htm; Pallavi Gogoi, "Is Circuit City Up for Sale?," *BusinessWeek.com,* April 8, 2008, http://www.businessweek.com/bwdaily/dnflash/content/apr 2008/db2008048_602083.htm; Pallavi Gogoi, "Is Circuit City Headed For a Blowout?" *BusinessWeek.com,* July 2, 2008, http://www.businessweek .com/bwdaily/dnflash/content/jul2008/db2008072_040726.htm.

242. Brian P. Knestout, "Hewlett-Packard: Separating Dr. Jekyll From Mr. Hyde," *Kiplinger's Personal Finance Magazine,* May 1999, 28; David P. Hamilton and Rebecca Blumenstein, "H-P Names Carly Fiorina, A Lucent Star, To Be CEO," *Wall Street Journal,* July 20, 1999; Hewlett-Packard Company, *2000 Annual Report* (Palo Alto: Hewlett-Packard Company, 2000); "HP Sends Letter to Shareowners on Value of Compaq Merger," *Business Wire,* January 18, 2002; Hewlett-Packard Company, *2002 Annual Report* (Palo Alto, CA: Hewlett-Packard Company, 2002); Carol J. Loomis, "Why Carly's Big Bet is Failing," *Fortune,* February 7, 2005, 50; Ben Elgin, "The Inside Story of Carly's Ouster," *BusinessWeek.com,* February 21, 2005, http://www.businessweek.com/technology/content/feb2005/tc20050210 _5176_tc119.htm; Carly Fiorina, *Tough Choices: A Memoir* (New York: Penguin Group, 2006); "If HP Just Wants to Cut Costs, It Picked the Right Guy," *Business Week,* May 2, 2005, 20.

243. Barnaby Feder, "Motorola Picks an Outsider to Be Its Chief Executive," *New York Times,* December 17, 2003; Laurie J. Flynn, "Motorola Replaces Chief With an Insider," *New York Times,* December 1, 2007; Motorola, Inc., *1999–2004 Summary Annual Reports* (Schaumburg, IL: Motorola, Inc., 2000– 2005); David Barboza, "Motorola Rolls Itself Over," *New York Times,* July 14, 1999; Roger O. Crockett, "A New Company Called Motorola," *Business Week,* April 17, 2000, 86; Roger O. Crockett, "Chris Galvin Shakes Things Up—Again," *Business Week,* May 28, 2001, 38; Roger O. Crockett, "Motorola," *Business Week,* July 16, 2001, 72; Roger O. Crockett, "Reinventing Motorola," *Business Week,* August 9, 2004, 98.

244. Claudia H. Deutsch, "A Giant Awakens, To Yawns: Is Rubbermaid Reacting Too Late?" *New York Times,* December 22, 1996; Susan Sowa, "Restructuring May Salvage Rubbermaid," *Rubber & Plastics News* 25, no. 10 (December 18, 1995): 7; Lornet Turnbull, "Ohio-Based Rubbermaid Inc. Heeds Findings from Consumer Focus Groups," *Akron Beacon Journal,* February 18, 1996.

245. Raju Narisetti, "Rubbermaid's Plan to Buy Graco Is Eclipsed by Poor Profit Forecast," *Wall Street Journal*, September 5, 1996; "Rubbermaid Sells Division To Newell," *Discount Store News*, May 19, 1997, 2; Glenn Gamboa, "Rubbermaid Corp. Is Proposing a Nice, Neat Solution," *Akron Beacon Journal*, August 6, 1997; "Rubbermaid to Consolidate Its Manufacturing, Distribution Operations," *Akron Beacon Journal*, January 22, 1998; "Rubbermaid: Giant With a Fearful Sense of Purpose," *DIY Week*, February 6, 1998, 22; Timothy Aeppel, "Rubbermaid Is On a Tear, Sweeping Away the Cobwebs," *Wall Street Journal*, September 8, 1998.

246. Michael J. Milne, "Scott Paper Is On a Roll," *Management Review* 77, no. 3 (March 1988): 37.

247. "Scott Paper Fights Back, At Last," *Business Week*, February 16, 1981, 104.

248. Bill Saporito, "Scott Isn't Lumbering Anymore," *Fortune*, September 30, 1985, 48; Michael J. Milne, "Scott Paper Is On a Roll," *Management Review* 77, no. 3 (March 1988): 37; "Scott Paper Co.—History," *Gale Business Resources*, 1990; "North American Earnings Plunge Again," *Pulp & Paper* 65, no. 13 (December 1991): 25; Stuart C. Gilson and Jeremy Cott, "Scott Paper Company," *Harvard Business School,* case study #9-296-048 (Boston: Harvard Business School Publishing, 1997); Albert J. Dunlap and Bob Andelman, *Mean Business: How I Save Bad Companies and Make Good Companies Great* (New York: Fireside, 1997), 11.

249. "Zenith Wants to Give the Boob Tube a Brain," *Business Week*, May 6, 1985, 71; Bob Tamarkin, "Zenith's New Hope," *Forbes*, March 31, 1980, 32; "Zenith May Lead the Way in the Video Revolution," *Business Week*, February 23, 1981, 94.

250. Robert Levering, Milton Moskowitz, and Michael Katz, "International Business Machines Corporation," *The 100 Best Companies to Work For In America* (New York: New American Library, 1984), 163; Jonathan Martin, "IBM: International Business Machines Corporation," *Information Technology*, no date, 147; David Kirkpatrick, "Breaking Up IBM," *Fortune*, July 27, 1992, 44; International Business Machines, *IBM 1992 Annual Report* (Armonk, NY: International Business Machines Corporation, 1993); International Business Machines, *IBM 1993 Annual Report* (Armonk, NY: International Business Machines Corporation, 1994).

251. Louis V. Gerstner, Jr., *Who Says Elephants Can't Dance? Inside IBM's Historic Turnaround* (New York: HarperCollins, 2002), dedication, 279.

252. Louis V. Gerstner, Jr., *Who Says Elephants Can't Dance? Inside IBM's Historic Turnaround* (New York: HarperCollins, 2002), 36, 54, 88, 102, 208; Judith H. Dobrzynski, "Rethinking IBM," *Business Week*, October 4, 1993, 86; Ira Sager, "IBM Reboots—Bit By Bit," *Business Week*, January 17, 1994, 82.

253. Louis V. Gerstner, Jr., *Who Says Elephants Can't Dance? Inside IBM's Historic Turnaround* (New York: HarperCollins, 2002), 44, 48, 50, 61, 63, 67, 72, 139, 204, 223.

254. Louis V. Gerstner, Jr., *Who Says Elephants Can't Dance? Inside IBM's Historic Turnaround* (New York: HarperCollins, 2002), 60, 132.

255. Louis V. Gerstner, Jr., *Who Says Elephants Can't Dance? Inside IBM's Historic Turnaround* (New York: HarperCollins, 2002), 1, 186, 201, 205, 221.

256. Louis V. Gerstner, Jr., *Who Says Elephants Can't Dance? Inside IBM's Historic Turnaround* (New York: HarperCollins, 2002), 20, 24, 36, 54, 57, 68–70, 92, 124, 139, 157, 165, 221; David Kirkpatrick, "Breaking Up IBM," *Fortune,* July 27, 1992, 44.

257. Louis V. Gerstner, Jr., *Who Says Elephants Can't Dance? Inside IBM's Historic Turnaround* (New York: HarperCollins, 2002), 95, 98, 182, 208, 280.

258. Louis V. Gerstner, Jr., *Who Says Elephants Can't Dance? Inside IBM's Historic Turnaround* (New York: HarperCollins, 2002), 66, 124, 188, 213.

259. Jeffrey L. Rodengen, *The Legend of Nucor* (Ft. Lauderdale, FL: Write Stuff, 1997), 63, 70, 82; Fortune 1000 rankings, from Fortune.com website, February 9, 2001; Nucor Corporation, *2004 Annual Report* (Charlotte, NC: Nucor Corporation, 2005), 3; Nucor Corporation, *2007 Annual Report* (Charlotte, NC: Nucor Corporation, 2008), 23; John P. McDermott, "Steelmaker Nucor Pushes Ahead with Growth Plan Despite Turbulent Times," *Post and Courier,* February 20, 2001; "Nucor CEO Resigns After Dispute Over Company Direction," *Industrial Maintenance & Plant Operation,* July 1999.

260. Vicki Lee Parker, "Steel Company Nucor Dominates North Carolina Economy," *News & Observer,* June 5, 2005; John P. McDermott, "Steelmaker Nucor Pushes Ahead with Growth Plan Despite Turbulent Times," *Post and Courier,* February 20, 2001; Nucor Corporation, *2008 Form 10-K* (Charlotte, NC: Nucor Corporation, 2008).

261. Norm Heikens, "Profitable Steelmakers in Indiana Point to Management, Pay Structure," *Indianapolis Star,* February 24, 2001; Nanette Byrnes and Michael Arndt, "The Art of Motivation," *Business Week,* May 1, 2006, 56; Susan Berfield, "The Best of 2006: Leaders," *Business Week,* December 28, 2006, 58; John P. McDermott, "Steelmaker Nucor Pushes Ahead with Growth Plan Despite Turbulent Times," *Post and Courier,* February 20, 2001; Jessica Marquez and Patrick J. Kiger, "Retooling Pay," *Workforce Management,* November 7, 2005, 1.

262. Nucor Corporation, *2000 Annual Report* (Charlotte, NC: Nucor Corporation, 2001).

263. Nucor Corporation, *2002 Annual Report* (Charlotte, NC: Nucor Corporation, 2003); Nucor Corporation, *2007 Annual Report* (Charlotte, NC: Nucor

Corporation, 2008); "Nucor Gets Loan," *Wall Street Journal*, March 3, 1972, 11; "Nucor's Big-Buck Incentives," *Business Week*, September 21, 1981, 42.

264. Sue Herera, "Nucor Corp.—CEO Interview," *CEO Wire,* December 2, 2003.

265. Nucor Corporation, *2005 Annual Report* (Charlotte, NC: Nucor Corporation, 2006).

266. Nucor Corporation, *2000 Annual Report* (Charlotte, NC: Nucor Corporation, 2001); Nucor Corporation, *2001 Annual Report* (Charlotte, NC: Nucor Corporation, 2002); Nucor Corporation, *2002 Annual Report* (Charlotte, NC: Nucor Corporation, 2003); "Up From the Scrap Heap," *Business Week*, July 21, 2003.

267. Jim Collins, *Good to Great: Why Some Companies Make the Leap . . . And Others Don't* (New York: HarperCollins Publishers, Inc., 2001), 107; Nucor Corporation, *2000 Annual Report* (Charlotte, NC: Nucor Corporation, 2001).

268. Nucor Corporation, *2000 Annual Report* (Charlotte, NC: Nucor Corporation, 2001); Nucor Corporation, *2001 Annual Report* (Charlotte, NC: Nucor Corporation, 2002).

269. Jessica Marquez and Patrick J. Kiger, "Retooling Pay," *Workforce Management,* November 7, 2005, 1; Anil K. Gupta and Vijay Govindarajan, "Knowledge Management's Social Dimension: Lessons from Nucor Steel," *Sloan Management Review* 42, no. 1 (Fall 2000); Susan J. Marks, "Incentives That Really Reward and Motivate," *Workforce* 80, no. 6 (June 2001): 108; Nanette Byrnes and Michael Arndt, "The Art of Motivation," *Business Week,* May 1, 2006, 56.

270. Nucor Corporation, *2001 Annual Report* (Charlotte, NC: Nucor Corporation, 2002); Nucor Corporation, *2003 Annual Report* (Charlotte, NC: Nucor Corporation, 2004).

271. Daniel DiMicco, "Steel Success Strategies XVI: Mini-Mill Takes Second Look—At Implementation," *American Metal Market*, June 20, 2001, 17A.

272. Nucor Corporation, *2001 Annual Report* (Charlotte, NC: Nucor Corporation, 2002).

273. Nucor Corporation, *2002 Annual Report* (Charlotte, NC: Nucor Corporation, 2003).

274. Nucor Corporation, *2004 Annual Report* (Charlotte, NC: Nucor Corporation, 2005).

275. Kathy Mulady, "Nordstrom Reports Earnings Nosedive: Disappointing Holiday Season, Economic Slump Blamed," *Seattle Post-Intelligencer*, February 23, 2001; Kathy Mulady, "Back In the Family," *Seattle Post-Intelligencer*, June 27, 2001; Rajiv Lal and Arar Han, "Nordstrom: The Turnaround," *Harvard Business School,* case study #9-505-051 (Boston: Harvard Business

School Publishing, 2005); Louise Lee, "Nordstrom Cleans Out Its Closets," *Business Week*, May 22, 2000, 105; Carol Tice, "Reinvention Rebuffed?" *Puget Sound Business Journal*, August 4, 2000, 1; Devon Spurgeon, "In Return to Power, The Nordstrom Family Finds A Pile of Problems," *Wall Street Journal*, September 8, 2000; Bill Kossen, "A Good Fit?" *Seattle Times*, May 29, 2001; "Can The Nordstroms Find the Right Style?" *Business Week*, July 30, 2001; Nordstrom, Inc., *Annual Report 2007* (Seattle: Nordstrom, Inc., 2008).

276. Rajiv Lal and Arar Han, "Nordstrom: The Turnaround," *Harvard Business School,* case study #9-505-051 (Boston: Harvard Business School Publishing, 2005); Kathy Mulady, "Nordstroms Again Take the Reins," *Seattle Post-Intelligencer*, September 1, 2000.

277. Kathy Mulady, "Another Move At Nordstrom," *Seattle Post-Intelligencer*, September 12, 2000; Rajiv Lal and Arar Han, "Nordstrom: The Turnaround," *Harvard Business School,* case study #9-505-051 (Boston: Harvard Business School Publishing, 2005); Robert Spector and Patrick McCarthy, *The Nordstrom Way to Customer Service Excellence* (Hoboken, NJ: John Wiley & Sons, Inc., 2005), 91, 144.

278. Bill Kossen, "A Good Fit?" *Seattle Times*, May 29, 2001; Nordstrom, Inc., *Annual Report 2002* (Seattle: Nordstrom, Inc., 2003); Rajiv Lal and Arar Han, "Nordstrom: The Turnaround," *Harvard Business School,* case study #9-505-051 (Boston: Harvard Business School Publishing, 2005).

279. Rajiv Lal and Arar Han, "Nordstrom: The Turnaround," *Harvard Business School,* case study #9-505-051 (Boston: Harvard Business School Publishing, 2005).

280. Rajiv Lal and Arar Han, "Nordstrom: The Turnaround," *Harvard Business School,* case study #9-505-051 (Boston: Harvard Business School Publishing, 2005); Carol Tice, "Bringing Nordstrom Back," *Puget Sound Business Journal*, December 26, 2003; Bill Kossen, "A Good Fit?" *Seattle Times*, May 29, 2001; Robert Spector and Patrick McCarthy, *The Nordstrom Way to Customer Service Excellence* (Hoboken, NJ: John Wiley & Sons, Inc., 2005), 143; Nordstrom, Inc., *Annual Report 2003* (Seattle: Nordstrom, Inc., 2004).

281. Nordstrom, Inc., *Annual Report 2002* (Seattle: Nordstrom, Inc., 2003); Bill Kossen, "A Good Fit?" *Seattle Times*, May 29, 2001; Nordstrom, Inc., *Annual Report 2003* (Seattle: Nordstrom, Inc., 2004), 11; Devon Spurgeon, "In Return to Power, The Nordstrom Family Finds A Pile of Problems," *Wall Street Journal*, September 8, 2000.

282. Rajiv Lal and Arar Han, "Nordstrom: The Turnaround," *Harvard Business School,* case study #9-505-051 (Boston: Harvard Business School Publishing, 2005).